"This book-album thing is a great idea. I can listen while I read, ignoring either what I'm reading or what I'm hearing, but it's *my choice*. I feel that Krista really respects my freedom. And let's face it, I would by anything Krista writes. I sometimes pay her just to send me emails. *Notes from the Bridge* will be better than an email (and cheaper by the word)."

> — Dr. Randall E. Auxier, author of *Time, Will and Purpose*; co-editor of *Bruce Springsteen and Philosophy* and *The Wizard of Oz and Philosophy*

"A book you say? Words and pictures affixed to pages, rendered betwixt covers? Odds bodkins, this Detor woman is mad! *Mad!!!*"

> -- Tom Matthews, screenwriter (*Mad City*), novelist (*Like We Care*) and freelance journalist (*Chicago Sun, Milwaukee Star, et.al.*)

"*Flat Earth Diary: Notes from the Bridge* provides readers a rare backstage pass to the creation of the album. Just be careful not to trip over the vodka bottles along the way. 'Cuz there's a ton. Seriously. They're everywhere. And while Detor's literary debut might not make its way on to the New York Times Bestseller list, if someone from New York buys a copy it will at least make its way to the city. And that's something..."

> — Dr. Rod C. Taylor, Author of *Music* (Fountainhead Press), and Asst. Prof. of Literature & Writing, Dept. of Literature, Writing & Philosophy, Tennessee State University

"Krista's writing makes me happy. She opens up my brain and heart like a monkey opening up a banana (from the other end.) It always feels so strangely good.."

– Sam Bartlett, Author of *Stuntology* (Workman Publishing), et.al.

"Krista Detor's lyrics blast the world apart, only to find wonder in each falling mote and shard.*"

- Nancy R. Hiller, Author, *A Home of Her Own* (Goodreads), et.al.

*[Editor's note: Ms. Hiller neglected to include a review of the book itself when forwarding the above quote. We're sure it's an oversight. Her representative declined comment].

It's an album. It's a book. It's two-two-two things in one. That Krista Detor, she really knows how to give value for money."

- Chris Nickson, Novelist
(The Richard Nottingham Novels, Emerald City),
Music Journalist.

"Friends—and I assume you are friends in spirit, at least, since, like me, you're attracted to the scintillating songs and capacious vision of Krista Detor—friends, I say, if you're looking for scientific knowledge about the shape of our planet and the workings of the cosmos, don't expect to find it in *Flat Earth Diary: Notes from the Bridge.* But if you're seeking wit, wisdom, low comedy, high art, and a questing spirit, you'll be richly rewarded by this lyrical book and splendid album."*

– Scott R. Sanders, Author
A Conservationist Manifesto (IU Press), et.al.

*(Editor's note: Mr. Sanders was not remunerated in any way, nor was he coerced into forwarding the above statement with fruit baskets and expensive champagne)

This book is dedicated to all of the Collaborators
on the *Flat Earth Diary* funding project.
In one month, you changed everything.
Thank you.

Copyright © 2013 by Krista I. Detor.

All rights reserved. This book or any portion thereof may not be reproduced or used in any manner whatsoever without the express written permission of the publisher, except for the use of brief quotations in a book review.

Printed in the United States of America

First Printing, 2013

ISBN 1492821640

Tightrope Records
P.O. Box 7814
Bloomington, IN 47407-7814

www.kristadetor.com

Cover art by Won Sook Kim
Back cover photo by Jim Krause
Scores transcribed by Peter Kienle

Foreward

"One of the proofs of the immortality of the soul is that myriads have believed it. They also believed the world was flat." – Mark Twain

In every important way, every song begins with a leap of faith. Whether or not Mark Twain believed in the existence of the human soul, it's hard for a songwriter to disregard the plausibility. Along the way – and this is in no way specific to me and my road-dogging experience* – we do leave little bits of them on barstools and in empty theatre seats. Our souls, I mean. We songwriters categorically believe that the soul exists, if for no other reason than the incessant whistling through the shadowy tatters of ours.** You need proof? Patti Smith might have a song for you. If not her, Leonard Cohen absolutely does. Maybe even me, if it comes to it.

The process of retrieving the song from this unknowable framework or space is the thing, though. It often feels to me like standing on the edge of the flat earth, leaning out slightly, feeling the pull of the nameless, dark – trying to make shapes in the murky silence, and then, inexplicably, leaping. People ask me about inspiration, how it comes about – what's the process. Sometimes it's alchemy. Black magic. I have no idea. Painters have such extraordinary descriptive language for their work. I wish I did. Or I'm glad I don't, because then I'd have to live up to it, and oh..

Magically, *Flat Earth Diary*, the album, came together on a 10-day sailing trip in Lake Huron's North Channel this past July. Some of the songs were already in existence, three of them written on the boat. When I boarded, the unrecorded album was planned to be titled, 'Box of Clouds,' and though the songs scheduled to be included were not all top picks for me (I'd written a lot in 4 years, but only a scant handful of songs I'd want in historical record). I was succumbing to pressure to produce something, anything, because I was keeping many people from doing their jobs by failing to produce anything since 2010 –namely booking agents who needed a new album to push U.S. and international tours.

So maybe it was the pressure, or maybe it was the water.

Maybe it was the space between myself and the incessant tug of online business and scheduled chicken feedings. Whatever the hocus-pocus, and for good, bad, or otherwise (I have yet to hear from the critics, but will soon enough), the album emerged in the title track, and the through-line instantly fell into place for me, as I floated through time, backward, pulling out mental snapshots of tinted black & white photos, feathered hats, tic-tac-toe on foggy windows..

But it's cumulative in nature, inspiration, I mean. The brain is said to process 0.1 quadrillion information bytes per second. A singular occurrence, image, or even sailing trip may be the tipping point for a creative output event, but myriad impressions come in prior and weave together the foundations of the vessels we launch. I thought I'd recall events, correspondence, artworks, the creations of friends and people whose work I admire that have inspired me along the way; conversations and all manner of miasma that lead to the songs that make up *Flat Earth Diary,* and you can draw your own conclusions.

Enjoy the ride, and when the wind gusts hit, grab a martini and ride it out with me to the end. There's bound to be an unforeseen plot twist. It would be sad if you gave up and missed it, and then there you'd be, wondering why my poker-playing uncle mysteriously disappeared.***

---

* See my friend, Carrie Newcomer's 'Speed of Soul' for a beautiful primer on the subject.
** Perhaps not 'categorically,' but definitely most likely
*** Disclaimer: I'm a songwriter, not a novelist. I know where the novelists drink. I can't abide whiskey in any form, so they generally ask me to sit at an adjacent table, or 'better yet, go play us something pretty.'

FLAT EARTH DIARY:
NOTES FROM THE BRIDGE

BY KRISTA DETOR

The   world   is   flat

everyone knows
who are you to say?

I've seen the
                edge

where the water goes
tu m bl ing
            into
                    space

        spi n n ing   off and

                                        away
                                        1/25/12

There are long periods in which nothing comes. Not a word, not a note. Nothing.

The world's a void and you'll never fill it, and whatever you had to say you've said, nearly as well as the next guy, and the

silence

is

deafening If you're me, you flip through old computer files in those frantic and grasping moments when the silence threatens to engulf you like so much tuna netting. I've titled my old files 'bullsh*t," "bullsh*t2," and "bullsh*t3." Yes, this is all horribly self-deprecating, but I don't know a writer that isn't, at moments, self-deprecating. Some of them churlishly, damn you. But in these files, I toss stanzas, lines, words that never found their way to a whole verse, let alone a whole song [and thusly were relegated to the bullsh*t files]. Maybe today they'll trigger something new – in this new context, on this new day, in this new pair of second-hand shoes, walking this old splintery floor.

Grasp. Grope. Maybe. (Generally, more silence follows).

One month after *Flat Earth Diary* (the album) was done and 'in the can,' I stumbled on the 1/25/12 stanza while gathering up the writings that spawned some of the songs. Was the notion of *Flat Earth* incubating for 18 months? Like an elephant baby or something

(I have no idea of the gestational period for elephant tots, but 18 months seems good)

This is the mysterious magic part. Because I don't know. I don't know the gestational period of baby elephants, or whether ideas incubate or are utterly spontaneous, given circumstance and happenstance and the ever-illusive roaming djinn of dejavu. I know that I tossed off a paragraph, and promptly forgot it. Probably because it was entirely forgettable, even set in the nifty style of ee cummings. And I might have been miffed.

But still, 18 months later, I was on a boat, no land in sight, reading Terry Pratchett's something or other for the 5th time and wanting more than anything to believe that the endless water poured off the edge of the flat earth to myriad stars, forever and ever amen.

Amen. And so it came to pass.

Cover Art: Courtesy of Won Sook Kim

Day One – July 2, 2013

I'm humming the theme song to *Gilligan's Island* as I type.

I've driven to Cheboygan, Michigan, to climb aboard the Traumfanger and set sail for 10 days with two good friends. Despite the worst boat name in the history of bad boat names (Traumfanger is German for 'dream catcher' - an all around lose-lose), I'm excited to board.

They bought the boat pre-named and are stuck with it, as, apparently, to change the name of a boat - and I am not making this up - a virgin has to urinate off the bow whilst the captain steers a series of figure 8s. This presents a number of logistical problems, including, and not limited to, incurring the wrath of The Kraken should you fail to execute the name-changing ritual precisely. They're practical people. Traumfanger it is.

I'll have my own small berth, and while I'll have to share the bed with a fairly aggressive cello, I'm looking forward to the escape from civilization into the wild blue unknown.

I need to compose. I need to finish an album. I'm beginning to consider this task akin to needing to lay the foundation for the Taj Mahal, without having procured a reputable marble dealer, not to mention several thousand camels.

In many important ways, I'm completely scr*wed with this looming deadline. I'm getting desperate.

It's okay, though. Jim's always got vodka.

CHAPTER 1: FERRYMAN'S DREAM

Buried in books

FERRYMAN'S DREAM began taking shape the

summer of 2011, the year I decided to actually read some of the classic literature on my shelves of books.

Having made a furtive commitment to NOTHING but science fiction as a high schooler, if I did leave Herbert, Asimov, Bradbury, Clarke and the like out among the stars, and touch down, grudgingly, to terra firma, I gobbled up Poe, then H.P. Lovecraft and then Stephen King & his alter-ego Bachman by the pulp pound, until the duo hit the dark, alcoholic years of *Christine*.. and then he/they lost me, until his/her essay, *On Writing*.

For whatever reason, I felt an instinctive need to refrain from fully earth-bound storyline for years. In college, I wandered happily into the magical realism of Marquez (though I read recently a grumpy critical smack of the term in relation to his work, as 'minimizing.' I still think there's immense value in its magic), Tom Robbins and the like. Middle Earth was unavoidable as I forayed into countless otherworldy adventures, including nearly everything Vonnegut wrote, Douglas Adams & Carl Hiaasen hilarity, (the list is long. I read all the time). And, when my sister introduced me to the one-foot-in, one-foot-out reality of Terry Prachett's *Discworld*, I stayed there, faithfully, for nearly a decade. It's a hard place to leave.

In between, occasional spaces were filled with endless books and collections of poetry, bestsellers suggested and/or given me by friends – Oprah Book Club stuff from my mom.*

I was blown away a couple of times by new works, but wasn't sure what, if anything, would stand up to the grand masters of Fitzgerald, Woolf, Salinger, Stein, Hemingway – a degree in Music and none of whom I'd read, so how would I know? But here's the thing –

I live in a house originally built at the turn of the last century. I love the period. I love the period pieces, I love the Victrola from Dave and the pump organ from Michael White. I love Modernism's flourishes. I looked up at the titles and realized that I was bound to love Fitzgerald (I did), Woolf (I did, once I learned how to un-focus my eyes - now I'm hooked), Stein (I did, though in a sprinting-through-jello kind of way) Salinger (I loved the boy that he was) and Hemingway (less than I had hoped. But I hold out hope).

My grandparents' childhood portraits hang on the walls, in hand-carved oval frames and the whole place feels like a museum. This, of course, has caused a couple of my more sensitive friends to conclude a hauntedness about it (the vintage, animated and slightly terrifying circus clown helps). But if it is haunted, it's by small dogs, tea-sippers on the porch swing, and children running up and down the stairs. In the summer of 2011, the only thing that haunted me and my house was a long line of unread books, floating just above the shelves.

2011 was a hard year of touring, and didn't feel specifically

---

*I admit it. I read the first two chapters of *Eat, Pray, Love* and when I actually went to Italy, ate anything I wanted. It was glorious.

fruitful. I'd released *Chocolate Paper Suites* the year before and had hoped to make more headway in the incessantly shifting, increasingly adolescent Folk Music market. I was reconsidering everything, including ever making another album or doing another show. I was exhausted by what felt to be endless head bashes against brick walls, grieving a little for what I didn't get from the critically successful, but still miles-under-the-radar *Chocolate Paper*, and, in a dark moment, before I'd read a word, the song started with a poem of frustration, rebellion, and surrender.

Seditious me
kd 7/26/11

Where the first spike was stayed
there a tunnel was made
Journeymen in coveralls
we were all there – we marked the calls
we stumbled blind into the mists
and lost our way, we beat walls with our fists
We breathed the black lung air
and fired blue flame, burning –
bled bright veins into shadows
while the earth went turning

Oh when and where did the lanterns glow?
We'd have grabbed them all
kept our voices low

Down here, over dark scarlet letters
I scrape my hands
and remember
I've disrupted other people's plans

But I look away from bell jars, weathered
and rumors tethered by
spikes and cries
toward a carousel of words and color
Lit like a cathedral, a holy spectacle
A holy signature
penned by Miro and Ives

I'll pack my bag, now
Pack up my exhibition
Pack up the trifles and the troubles
that grumble and glisten

It's bygone now, and girly-show girls
are dressed in old feathers
and old rambler leather
and it's the same show, playing over and over

But somebody in a ferryman's dream
knew just what I mean
and believed it was true
that the ending is simple:
The only one that crosses is you.

Into the blue light and out of it
Oh, hear the shout of it.
One word of truth, sing me one
Only one

And it won't be *sedition*
Up there in the sun

The Poets The Poets

The writers I've known over the years, whose words
have influenced my outcomes.

Hello filtered imagery
hello reconstruction, reclassification
Goodbye to what I knew
Figuratively? No.
Just goodbye.
It ain't comin' back, baby.

       (the ghosts
             lurk)

- Robert J. Weber Jr.

FERRYMAN'S DREAM

kd   3/2012

I am buried in books I don't read
You say I am lazy and mean – I can be mean
Cause I don't like to stay out too late
Don't wanna go on a blind date
I'm bored with the war - the strategic advances
So I'm packing it in and I'll take my chances

It's not that you've done something wrong
Or that I got shot in a song - shot in a song
It's just that it's gotten me low
this sedition with trials yet to go
I've heard your confession –
But mine's still locked in a drawer
So I'm packing it in and I swear to you I will hear no more

You swing from the limbs of the tree
And smile as you're flying by me
I'm winded just watching …

we stumble blind into the mists
Lose our way, beat the walls with our fists - beat the walls
Breathe in the black lung air
Fire flame that burns blue up in there
Tap the bright vein in darkness
While the world goes turning -
But I'm packing it in,
Even though the blue flame is still burning

Yeah, I'll pack my bag now
Pack up my exhibition
Pack up the trifles and the troubles
that grumble and glisten, listen:

Someone in a ferryman's dream
knew fully well what I mean – knew what I mean

beyond wuthering weather, an old scarlet letter
knew what I believe to be true
that the ending is simple: Nobody crosses but you.

So I'll look away from the bell jars
stacked up like old railroad cars -
toward carousels colored in words
and ellipticals like holy spectacles
painted in miracle blue.... like I saw your eyes
there with Miro & Ives
I'm packing it in
Maybe get lucky, have two lives

Ferryman's Dream

by Krista Detor

Copyright © 2013 by Krista Detor, Tightrope Publishing

Verse 3

watch-ing......... We stum-ble blind in - to the mists Lose our way, beat the walls with our fists Beat the walls...... Breathe in the black lung air Fire flame that burns blue up in there Tap the bright vein in dark-ness While the world goes turn - ing......... But I'm pack-ing it in, Ev-en though the blue flame is still bur - n-ing..............

Instrumental

(violin)

Yeah,

Chorus 2

I'll pack my bag now........ Pack up my ex - hi - bi - tion Pack up the trif - les and the

Verse 4

troub-les that grum-ble and glist-en...... list-en...... Some - one in a fer-ry-man's dream

knew ful-ly well what I mean knew what I mean be-yond wuth-er-ing wea-ther, an old scar-let let-ter knew

what I be-lieve to be true that the end-ing is sim-ple No-bo-dy cros-ses but you So

Chorus 3

I'll look a-way from the bell jars Stacked up like old rail-road cars To-ward car-ou-sels col-ored in

words and el-lip-ti-cals like ho-ly spec-tac-les paint-ed in mir-a-cle blue like I saw your eyes

there with Mi-ro and Ives I'm pack-ing it in May-be I am luck-y get two lives

18

"May stem-rot and hoof-stink and demons stay far from your garden gate…"

Bloomington author and spoken-word performer, Arbutus Cunningham is a friend and collaborator. She's inspired me from the moment I heard her read, June of 1999, on WFHB, the community radio station here in Bloomington, where she hosts a morning show. We've corresponded over the years, occasionally with an actual purpose.

From: Arbutus Cunningham
To: Krista Detor
Sent: Mon, October 31, 2011 1:33:15 PM
Subject: I repent the snark.

Dear Boris,

I learned 2 new words before 8 this morning (*lanugo,* soft wooly hair that covers the human fetus, and some other mammals; *nutation,* a vibratory motion of the earth's axis like the nodding of a top) and am as a consequence of this industry steeped in virtue. Also hooked the fin of a new story, quite insane, which I hope to net before 3.

Am abashed I did not say something even remotely pleasant yesterday, as in "I am sorry you do not feel well" or even "thanks for getting the outline together for the December show" (about which--the show, not the outline--all my lanugo stands on end; I nutate along my axis). May moths not eat your burka; may you flourish in music; may your children thrive; may stem-rot and hoof-stink and demons stay far from your garden gate.

Natasha

Dear Natasha –

It occurs to me that I may be allergic to nutation. This would explain why nothing about my personal cosmology is aligned. I fear the problem must be systemic sensitivity..

Should I die of noddling whilst handing out candy to teenagers, allow no parade but rather I only want that man formerly known as Cat Stevens to sing 'Moonshadow' and let it be done with that. Since he likely won't take off his scimitar, nor his wife's full burka, I'll have to settle for The Mormon Tabernacle Choir.

Thanks for making the arrangements.

Signed,
Josephina Smith Ab-El KofiAnnan

Dear Ms. Ab-El Gaddafi

You poor vibratory female shrouded in dark heavy wool garments of a tubular shape. I will get right on those arrangements.

I have deleted some snarky lines; I don't like anyone today. The Mormon Tabernacle Choir is unavailable for some months: their director, predicting a Romney nomination, contemplates a move to the Rose Garden. Which, don't forget, I never promised you.
Snarkina Frowst.

Day Two – July 3, 2013

We're heading across Lake Huron today, to a place called Detour Village, aptly enough, following a night at the marina and a fairly lackluster fried meal of some sort in town.

Mayflies are everywhere. Poor little buggers. In a scant 24 hours they have to learn all the latest moves, get fitted for the tux, marry, mate and die. Well, many of them here in Cheboygan won't make as far as the school dance, even. As we drove to pick up groceries, the sound of the bugs crunching was the scritch of small bubble wrap pops. Millions upon millions of mayflies covered the boat, the town, and the roads. Ssssscccrrrriiiittttcccch. - A little distressing. But I can't afford to think on these things long. I get caught up in existential notions that my brain has proven too sluggish to fully process. And it's still too early to drink.

As soon as the boat gets hosed off, we untie and set sail. Today will be a 12-hour haul. The weather is actually perfect. Anne apologizes for the length of the trip, as if the notion of 12 hours out of cell phone range on calm blue water 'neath glowy Mr. Sunshine is an inconvenience.

But, she says, there are amazing coves and islands, utterly isolated from the maddening melee of humanity, and wait til I see it. Maybe I'll feel like myself again by the time we get to paradise. I mean Canada.

CHAPTER 2: BELLE OF THE BALL

Victor Wooten recording Belle of the Ball, August 15, 2013

BELLE OF THE BALL came to fruition following

a dinner with Victor Wooten in the early autumn of 2012. He'd come to town to play a show at The Bluebird and he and I have a mutual good friend in Rod Taylor, who arranged the meeting.

We talked about his life on the road, life in the business, just life. I was struck, most profoundly, with his references to 'discipline' – not only in the realm of music, but in general. Something in the way he spoke the word - as if discipline were the net under the trapeze, the insulated coat in a blizzard; as if discipline were the boat on the open sea. What his references *didn't* hold were notions *I'd* assigned discipline: grueling task master, 5th grade teacher with the hand-smacking ruler, and the incessantly whining voice in the back of my head reminding me that I haven't meaningfully played scales or arpeggios since music school and why would any rational person want to start any of that horrible stuff at this late date. (Squirrel!)

But there he was, at sound check, with his extraordinary band, and Victor's discipline was a spatial anomaly, enveloping and emanating from him like pulses of blue-white light. I was so taken with what I saw and felt while he played that I actually painted it the next day. Badly.* Still, I like to think I captured something of the transcendence. I suppose I did, if for no one other than myself. Regardless, he locked a new notion of discipline into my pumpkin head. In small ways since, I've acted on it, even if I've yet to play a single scale.

That's not the point.

Maybe somewhere that *is* the point.

I don't know. I do know that now, here, the point is that he's also an incredibly personable, kind and straight-forward man. In my estimation, combined, these qualities make up the best of what we humans can hope to be. And other songwriters will tell you – being in the presence of artistry inspires you to want to jump into the slipstream of it, leap into the star field of it. Write the song of it.

I leapt.

Little tiny net.

---

*I'm a songwriter, not a painter. I know where the painters drink and I've been notified that until I can write a decent descriptive paragraph about the music I make, I'll need to take my angst elsewhere.

I don't know what about Victor made me want to dabble with fairy tale twists, but I started with Red Riding Hood.

Red Riding Hood   kd 10/12

My man up and died so I never brush my hair
And I never wonder what in the world I'm gonna wear
to the royal ball.
They can keep the shoes and all.

Just bring me something pretty in a basket
something pretty in a basket –
like a pie, like a pie
But when you see me, don't you
say a thing about my eye

Yes, bring me something pretty in a basket
Something pretty in a basket
Like a rose
Like a rose
And when you see me, don't you say
A thing about my great big nose

Where was everybody when the woodcutter came
chopping at my door
The sound of the trees falling, the trees falling and I couldn't
take it any more
So I chased him from my woods
I did the thing I thought I should
And it is quiet now except for the birds
And simply put, I've tired of the things
That can be put to words

So bring me something pretty in a basket
Something pretty in a basket
Like a lavendar wreath
pretty wreath
And when you see me, don't you say
A thing about my long sharp teeth

Cinderella's shoes showed up in Red Riding Hood's granny's
tale, shortly followed by Cinderella herself.

God Save the King   kd 11/2012
(Cinderella Revisited)

It was my glass slipper -
chipped and splintered there upon the step.
So what, you found it, barely knew it - that I'd ever fit into it

On the way to what I'd come
to see myself as, in that dress -
right there I found it even if you and I did dance around it:

Kingdom's slow in coming
but I've heard you call it out
to nameless faces at the fences -
full of hope - more full of doubt

They wait for what is offered -
for what is theirs alone
but who will sing, *God save the King*
when Kingdom's coming, trumpets sounding?

Sons of pretty mothers
Go sailing out to sea
And who will sing, *God save the king*
When no one's here with me

Oh, I'd go back to Kansas
Before houses sprouted there -
Kingdom come was miles away
And light was every, light was everywhere

And then I remembered a title and a handful of stanzas in the bullsh*t3 file. A scrappy waltz, part twisted childhood ditty, part bile.* Set in a dark 6/8 to a stolen bass line from Brahms' Ballades. Too dark even for me to fully carry forward.

Tisket-Tasket   kd 03/11

You're from someplace where the suitors all call with hibiscus
bouquets for the **Belle of the Ball**
where dogs aren't howling all through the whole night
and everyone loves when you cheat in a fight
yes they do (in the mind of no other but you)

Maybe you loved him a long time before
while you traveled the world, flying from door to door -
when the spotlight was sweet, kept you out of the shadow
and off of your feet, far away from what you

---

*To quote my friend, songwriter Kenny White: "You can do a lot with bitterness."

just might do   (At the hands of no other but you)
So, what did you think after years of your asking
at least once a week to be tisketing, tasketing –

to skip down the road on your own
with a basket of cards for a lover who never existed?

You wanted escape, yeah and you got your freedom and
when you thought otherwise, then did you see him - a man
who'd put up with your wanton temerity?
Too late to turn back, oh no, he was gone, you see?
(It's true. far away from no other but you)

Do you see all the faces, all of those images
lit by the fires burning under the bridges
while you flaunt another tarnishing ring?
But who listens to you while the mockingbirds
sing? No one listens to **bluejays**
while mockingbirds sing.

Meanwhile, American politics were hitting a seemingly all-time low as we geared for the big election; an amoral group of pantywaists in a grid-locked 2-party catastrophe, cow-towing to all manner of greasy special interest while the whole nation suffered. Good people losing their homes, losing their jobs, unions were falling; pundits pandering to misinformation, ignorance and fear, and not a shred of honor to be found anywhere. Small beams of light shot up here and there – in the virally-spreading TED talks, the Occupy move -

ment, progressives in main-stream media once in a while, even. But not enough to override the side show that our elected leaders had made of the democratic process.

Okay, I've read enough Hunter S. Thompson to know that this is little more than "business as usual" - but that's a cynical view that he didn't survive. I try to be hopeful, though some days I wonder if I'll survive mine. And yes, I know that cynicism is tedious and common - an utter failure of imagination. But I'm drawn that way, despite valiant efforts at manufacture of a sunny disposition. When *Belle of the Ball* found its way to solidity, I was deep in the dark waters. The world was watching the blood sport of our political gladiator games; stressing another war, an Iranian invasion? I wasn't sure at all who I'd vote for. For the first time, if I'd vote at all.

It seemed to me that the system was crumbling around me, hemorrhaging internally, while the blood, bones and toxic waste of war-based economy at the hands of special interest had poisoned all of the ground water, all of the good air, stealing the soul of the nation and the future of its children. And I could just hear it - the low murmur in the dark, the song of the mothers of the dead, the calls for justice, the slow chant, like a heartbeat: *Enough. Enough. Enough.* I walked by David one night, playing a guitar riff that echoed the heartbeat I heard, and the song was born.

BELLE OF THE BALL

Words & Music by Krista Detor   Music by David Weber 03/12

Listen now – there comes a call
it seems I was the Belle of the Ball
I left a shoe behind me, and somebody came to find me
now I carry on behind a wall

And here they march, armor on
a battle cry is rising with the dawn
another war before him, at the court they all adore him,
the will of The Almighty leads him on

> *Kingdom's slow in coming*
> *but signs are all around*
> *so who will sing, 'God save the King'*
> *when Kingdom's coming, walls are tumbling down?*

At the gate, does he know?
they wait for any scrap that he might throw
but is that hunger in their eyes or
golden dresses they despise?
I remember that I used to know

The fires, does he see?
they watch beneath the bridges, warily
and while he flaunts a golden ring,
the mockingbirds begin to sing
I remember blue birds sang to me

Will they call for my head -
I'm not the kind of girl to cry about what is said
but I am aware of all the battles, all rows of empty saddles
all the songs of the mothers of the dead

Kingdom's slow in coming
but signs are all around
so who will sing, 'God save the King'
when Kingdom's coming down?

The songs of pretty mothers
go darkly to the sea
and who will sing, 'God save the king'
when darkness falls on me?

Oh, I'd go back to Kansas
before houses landed there
Kingdom Come was worlds away
and light was everywhere, everywhere

BELLE OF THE BALL

by Krista Detor & Dave Weber

copyright © 2013 by Krista Detor. Tightrope Publishing

VERSE 3

gate, does he know? they wait for an - y scrap that he __ might throw but is that hun - ger in __ their

eyes or gold - en dres - ses they de - spise? I re - mem - ber I used to know The

VERSE 4

fires, does he see? they watch be - neath the bridg - es, wa - ri - ly and while he flaunts a gold - en

ring, the mock - ing - birds be - gin __ to sing I re - mem - ber blue birds sang to me __

CHORUS

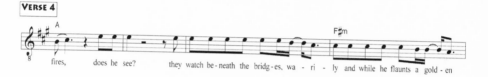

King-dom's slow in com - ing __ but signs are all a - round __ so who will sing, 'God save

... the King' when King - dom's com - ing, walls __ are tumbl - ing down? __

(viola)

Will they

copyright © 2013 by Krista Detor. Tightrope Publishing

copyright © 2013 by Krista Detor. Tightrope Publishing

38

Ext. Chorus 2

songs of pret - ty moth - ers Go dark - ly to the sea___ And

who will sing, 'God save___ the King'___ When dark - ness falls on me? Oh,

Ext. Chorus 2

I'd go back to Kan - sas Be - fore hous - es land - ed there___ King - dom Come was worlds

___ a - way___ And light___ was ev - 'ry - where___ ev - 'ry - where___ (fade out, bass fills)

copyright © 2013 by Krista Detor. Tightrope Publishing

The Poets

The Poets

We don't want your handouts, Mister
we don't want no charity
want to work and stay together
pick the fruit, land of the free

- Tim Grimm, *The People's Highway*

Now the zoo's in ruins
no one is spared
not the American bald eagle,
not the Russian bear
children would have cried
if any had survived
the bombing of the Berlin zoo

- Tom Roznowski, *The Bombing of the Berlin Zoo*

Day Three – July 4, 2013

I'm in Canada for the 4ᵗʰ of July.

I'm not sure how to follow that sentence, other than to state the obvious: There will be no fireworks.

Capt. Jim stopped in Blind River to call Canadian customs and notify them that I am on board. He and Anne have some sort of 'All Access Pass' to Canadian waters, but they cleared some levels of NSA and international security for that privilege. Not me. There was a time, not long ago, when this would not have been an issue. The days of open borders are behind us just now. Maybe they'll return by the last installment of 'The Hobbit.' [Assuming that the last installment of 'The Hobbit' doesn't take 90 years and include another 16-hour dwarves-ransacking-the-kitchen scene. Aside from the folks that make the annual treks to Comic Con and the like, there maybe couldn't be a bigger LOTR fan than me. But come on. Dragging minutia out and stretching it like taffy in order to cash in on multiple movie releases is only good capitalism. Not good movie making.]

But I digress. I'm in Canada and I feel awake for the first time in a while. The weather is pristine so far. Beyond good. We sailed part of the way across, motored the other, depending on winds and whim.

Reading the NYT Magazine, I ran across a great line: '.. he wrote it all down and then imploded..'

Here's hoping I at least get the chance to write it all down first.

CHAPTER 3: JUST BECAUSE

Photo by Jim Krause, courtesy of Bloom Magazine

JUST BECAUSE came as a direct result of an artificial

deadline. I'd asked my friend, Rod, a professor at Stanford at the time, to impose it, because I was dry. Dead dry. Nothing to write, nothing to say - in one of those piteous states of self-recrimination and prostrations that make me most likely impossible to live with. I work well under deadline - just not deadlines of my own mandate. I needed outside help from someone who commands a certain authority.

"Just say it," I said on the phone. "Say 'you have 10 days to write an album.'"

"Er. Okay," he replied, in good humor. "You have 10 days to write an album."

"Thanks," I said, and hung up. Over the next three hours I wrote *Just Because*, start to finish, with the help of an existing song that never found a voice. Ridiculous, I know. I make no excuse because there I was – sitting at my piano, an artificial deadline in the back of my head, and it worked. I got a song. Not an album, but still.

It was raining in January - the day before my birthday and snow was melting as it slid down the tree trunk. I have small windows in the studio where I write and I can see little more than trees, leaves, and sometimes in spring, woodpeckers.

Just above the studio is a bedroom. I remember the day I got married, as guests were arriving for the ceremony, taking seats in the back field near the huge, rented white tent that would nearly catch fire late in the evening, as the fireworks came too close, falling like tiny meteors everywhere. And how I'd secretly loved it – millions of tiny droplets of fire falling everywhere, ash floating down and landing in my hair against a backdrop of black sky and stars. It was no catastrophe, happily. The summer had been rain-soaked.

I stood in the window, watching guests arrive, looking out at the blackening sky – a mighty storm was threatening. I tell myself that I willed the clouds away. I stood, silent, imagining them moving east, and they did. No rain fell. Bright blue sky all day and not a drop into the night. I take full credit. Recalling the day, the song came easily, with the help of another that never found a melody line.

There's a long piece of pine board fence that wedding guests wrote wishes on, even painted on. The weather has worn away much of the writing, but the wedding wall remains, far and beyond the finish line.

Who am I to say?

[em F   (7ths) 40's riff –
   I IV trad Chorus]

It wasn't set in stone
the bluebell at her ear
the statues in the pond
the twirling statue girls
the murmur and the stir
the night you brought me here

CH: So who am I to say
what will or will not last
when what there is today
blooms in the distant past

It wasn't in the cards
this languid twist of fate
the painted pine board fence
painted a dogwood tree
in hazel **green,** by hand
the way you made me wait

So who am I to say
what will or will not be
when what there is today
is *Stardust* reverie

It wasn't what was planned
the barrels filled with rain
the mast tied to the barn
the sailboat mast you found
the amber barley grass
that hid the hull's remain
So who am I to say
what will or will not do

when what there is today
is rust and rain and you

This wasn't what I thought
would be the **lingering** line
the figure-skating girls
the figures on the pond
in pallid, lily white
the way you made them mine

So who am I to say
what will or will not go
when what there is today
is all I need to know

JUST BECAUSE

krista detor 1/11/13

Branches are so solemn
in the winter, always call them 'sticks in gray'
Snow is melting off them
in the mud, we're back to Autumn for a day

> But it was warm, when you said it
> you bet it was the finest minute, yes it was

> *just because we both were there*
> *just because she had a bluebell in her hair*
> *and just because the sun did shine*
> *I could keep on, far and beyond the finish line*

On the pine board fence, there are only shadows left of
painted birds
Only few have seen, there in ink and apple green,
the pretty words

> But it was warm, when they painted -
> they colored in the finest minute, yes it was
> *just because we both were there*
> *just because she had a bluebell in her hair*
> *and just because the sun did shine*
> *I could keep on, far and beyond the finish line*

It wasn't what was planned
so I tied it to my hand like a kite on a string
And then let it go, and I might never know –
but against the sun, the shadow always, always lingering

I hear the murmur and the stir
I answer to the quiet, 'rest a while'
If only while the water falls,
I dream of dancing down the halls and smile, smile, smile,
I smile, smile,

I smile, when we dance it –
the music and the finest minute, yes it was
> *just because we both were there*
> *just because she had a bluebell in her hair*
> *and just because the sun did shine*
> *I could keep on, far and beyond the finish line*

I smile, smile, smile…
far and beyond the finish line.

JUST BECAUSE

by Krista Detor

copyright © 2013 by Krista Detor. Tightrope Publishing

CHORUS

copyright © 2013 by Krista Detor, Tightrope Publishing

54

-ways lin-ger-ing___ I hear the mur-mur and the___ stir I

ans-wer to___ the quiet, 'rest a while' If on-ly while the wa-ter falls, I dream of danc-ing down the halls and

smile, smile, smile, I smile, smile I - a-ye,___ I___ smile while we danced

___ it___ the mus-ic and the fin-est min-ute, yes it___ was just be-cause___ we both were

there, just be-cause___ she had a blue-bell in her hair___ and just be-cause the___ sun did shine,

___ I___ could keep on far and be-yond the fin-ish line___ I smile, smile smile___

___far and be-yond the fin-ish line

copyright © 2013 by Krista Detor, Tightrope Publishing

IT'S HAIKU FRIDAY!

Fleeing the Nazgul
Frodo donned the ring and POOF!
Fictional regret
8/2011

It's Limerick Wednesday!

I ask, was the rockets' red glare
candy apple or steak that's cooked rare?
You see, there's a reason:
in honor of the season
I'm thinking of dying my hair
7/4/2012

Day FOUR – July 5, 2013

We've docked at Turnbull Island, and I got a song!

Jim & Anne went exploring in the dinghy and I had the boat to myself. Surrounded by so much water, and the small islands in the cove we've anchored at, the world could be flat for all I know. And me sitting here making journal entries.

And there it was: Flat Earth Diary. Where the hell did that come from? Suddenly, it's a song. Anne told me about an island in the Detroit River yesterday, covered in swans. The image stuck and I went pouring through b*llshit files and then remembered the bits of poetry I wrote down, from readings at Jenny Candor's* tribute a couple of months prior. Great lines – 'naked at the margin,' 'clouds crashing into the pond.' Two hours and the whole thing had poured onto the computer screen. I even grabbed the NYT line about implosion. A friend in the UK said, recently, 'Talent borrows. Genius steals.' I told him, 'Good. Now I don't feel so bad.' He laughed. (Not an easy feat making an Englishman chuckle).

Finally. Words again. I thought I was done for good. I can hear the general melody. I'll get them to break out the cello and guitar later and I'll rough it out.

How unseemly would it be for me to change the album title? Because THIS could be the title track. I think I have a couple of more songs in me, even. Time to sift through what's already going to make the album, and see what holes need to be filled. But ater.

For now, I'm going to swim to the shore. Not the brightest thing to do with no one in sight, but what the hell. It's not like there are sharks.

---

*Jenny Candor is a wonderful poet and host of the radio show, 'The Linen of Words.'

60

CHAPTER 4: RED VELVET BOX

The red velvet box from my grandmother

RED VELVET BOX.

It's a holiday song. It's not a holiday song. It didn't start as a holiday song, but it made a brief appearance as a holiday song. Now it's once again lost the sleigh bells, closer to its original roots. It was easy - they become noon bells, and Voila! I mean No-Ho-Ho! I mean.. I guess I didn't want it contained to playing only in the month of December.

It's gone through more incarnations than the Dalai Lama, but did settle into its current non-holiday form by way of the holidays – I needed another song for the annual holiday show that I do. I had some unrealized variations in the b*llshit files, so I grabbed everything up one day, and re-tooled it.

My grandmother's era of the 40s is its setting. At her place, I'd watch Audie Murphy movies, Gunsmoke re-runs, Lawrence Welk, Abbott & Costello and The Little Rascals. Re-runs. Let's just be clear on that – RE-Runs. But in the living room where we watched the shows on her little color TV with the antennae on top and the clickety-clickety remote control, were countless pictures of 'the old days,' girls with pin-curled hairdos, modest dresses, dapper young men with suits and ties. *Oh what it time it was, it was.. a time.* I suspect the 60s and 70s must have been something of a shock to her system, such chaos and disregard for convention - though she did seem to fully embrace the 'psychedelic' color schema: Her trailer was a wash of rainbow colors punctuated by doilies, figurines and 'crazy quilts' made from the tail ends of leftover bolts of fabric.

She gave me a red velvet box one year. There were finger insertions in the bottom. When you opened the box, three little mouse puppets covered your fingers. And then, of course, you made them dance, delightedly. Naturally, I pretended they were real and named them all. They were singing mice.*

I still have the box. It comes out at the holidays, along with the sock monkey and the red and white crocheted garland.

---

*Yes. I was *that* kid.

Potted Plants   *KDetor, 02/11*

There are countless potted plants on the landing. Three rickety steps lead to an array of bright lime greens and blues, chipped and rusted pots and receptacles - scavenged from Woolworth's clearance and years-old garage sales. - all containing full, bushy, spidery and cactussy, ferny things, given from one woman to the next as a single stem in a jar of water, at one time or another. My grandmother has the green thumb, allright. In the corner of the deck, a small, white (decorative?) toilet holds in its bowl a huge, hearty philodendron, whose tendrils wrap around the railings as it spreads, patiently, outward toward the other plants; the crowning display lit by the bright green astro-turf covering the porch.

It's Sunday and we'll gather at my grandma Wilma's trailer, like we always gather, with the aunts, uncles and cousins, and the men will drink beer from cans while the women sip Sanka and smoke cigarettes. *Gunsmoke* and *Lawrence Welk* re-runs will be on the small TV (color TV, a birthday gift from her children) and a cooler full of generic "pop" will be outside the door: Citrus-Up and Mr. Pepper and Orange Blast and the like.

'What's that smell?' asks my friend, a holdover from the Saturday sleepover, pinching her nostrils together, grimacing. "Lutefisk," I say. "I think it's Norwegian for 'boiled mop.'"

Let the feast begin.

At her wake, years later - the cousins will speak of my grandmother's culinary legacy - cakes, pies, breads and something called 'lefsa,' with such fondness that I think, perhaps, I knew an entirely different grandmother with completely different cooking skills.

"The lefsa - oh, the yummy lefsa...," a cousin waxes, a cup of coffee steaming up her glasses. In actuality, lefsa is a cold potato tortilla of sorts (more flavor being had by running downhill with your mouth open, as it's said) that my brother and childhood cousins slathered with margarine and sugar and rolled up like a poster. Thus creating a cold, crunchy, oily, sweet, ghastly potato tube that they munched, gleefully, while I watched *Gunsmoke* reruns and left my corporeal body.

The stuff apparently takes all day and an army of aunts to make. I would, on occasion, under threat of my mother to partake of the unholy tube, glob on approximately ½ a jar of crunchy Jif peanut butter and heat the whole mess in the microwave. With a big enough glass of milk, it was palatable, I suppose, in a gloppy, drippy, potatoey way.

"Sorry", I say to the table full of cousins, "I was there, I lived it. Lefsa should only be used to subvert our enemies; that and lutefisk. Yuck. And I mean, come on! When did any one of you EVER slice a piece of Grandma's bread that didn't crumble into dry little chunks all over your plate? She didn't believe in salt or... or..." I stop, mid-sentence as an in-law giggles, knowingly, eyes averted, while the room quiets and the dishwashing army aunts stop, mid-scrub, and turn as one to glower at the blasphemer.

But I know the truth. I'm the only one here with the palette to discern that bread shouldn't crumble and that lefsa should only be eaten when everything, including the miracle whip, is gone. Still, I miss my grandmother and would gladly eat the lefsa if she were here to make it.

I'll always pass on the lutefisk.

The Road to Red Velvet

Red Velvet Box started out as a lament of love lost. Luckily, later it had a sense of humor about things.

Go on and bury my heart   kd 02/09

Go on and bury my heart 'neath the sycamore
there in the shade
where it's a cool and I adore the garden gate
far from here and romance
Bury my heart and maybe I'll stand a chance

Go on and bury my heart with the cotton candy
and bourbon pie from the jack-a-dandy
anything else that reminds me of you
Bury my heart maybe I'll know what to do
I've emptied out my pockets for some scrap remaining
Tossed it all out - like the old refraining
pitter patter of the matter - settling up with the maitre'd

I'll make my way, no, no don't you worry
the cab is out front and it's in a hurry
only room for one - but where will the driver take me?

Go on and bury my heart with a tootsie roll
your cuban cigar in a shallow hole
the red velvet box - with the sweet little ring
Bury my heart and I won't feel a thing

Red Velvet Box

by Krista Detor

Baby, make it a heart when you're thinking of me
Wrap it up in cotton candy like the jack-a-dandy
at the carnival by the sea

Oh, make it a heart when the snow starts to fall
Take the bow from the gown
when we were out on the town -
champagne kisses and all

And in the red velvet box, baby
Make my wishes come true
Oh, make it heart, baby, heart -
The one that belongs to you

Go on and make it a heart 'neath the sycamore tree
Swinging on the garden gate when the night was getting late
and we had no place to be

All I want is a heart when the noon bell rings
and if you give me your heart, baby,
I will never ever, never need another thing

Cause you know that I've been good, baby
Nobody better than me
I want a star by my name
nobody else the same for you will ever be

I've emptied out my pockets for
some scrap remaining
tossed it all out like the old refraining
pitter patter of the matter,
settling up with the Maitre-D

I'll make my way, no no,
no, don't you worry
cab's out front and he's in a hurry -
Knows I got date underneath a sycamore tree

Cause all the boys that I knew
With bourbon pie and money, too -
sugar plums nice and sweet
I left 'em standing in the street
'cause they got nothing on you

And in the red velvet box, baby, box baby
Maybe a sweet little ring
Oh if you give me your heart, baby
I will never ever, never need another thing

RED VELVET BOX

by Krista Detor & Dave Weber

copyright © 2013 by Krista Detor. Tightrope Publishing

copyright © 2013 by Krista Detor. Tightrope Publishing

up with the Mai-tre-D_____ I'll make my way,_____ no, no, no, don't you wor-ry

D | G Ab A Bb B | E9 Eb9 D9 C#9 | Am | B7

cab's out front and he's in a hur-ry knows I got a date un-der-neath the sy-ca-more tree, la-la-

Em /D# | Em/D C#ø | Am7 | F#

VERSE 5

la

B | B Bb A | A AbG F#7#9 D7 | 'Cause all the boys that I knew | G

(Cha-cha)

G

With bour-bon pie and mo-ney, too su-gar plums nice and sweet I left 'em stand-ing in the

CHORUS

D7 | G | Am

street 'cause they go no-thing on you_____ And In the red vel-vet box, ba-by, box, ba-by

A | Em7 | Am

May-be a sweet lit-tle ring_____ Oh, if you give me your heart,_____ I will ne-ver ev-er,

copyright © 2013 by Krista Detor. Tightrope Publishing

CHORUS

ev-er need a-no-ther thing......... la-la-la-la-la And in the red vel-vet box, ba-by, box ,ba-by May-be a sweet lit-tle

ring Oh, if you give me your heart I ne-ver, ev-er, ev-er, ne-ver need a-no-ther thing la-la-la-la-la

la-la-la-la-la-la la-la-la-la-la la-la-la-la-la-la la-la-la-la-la la-la-la-la-la-la la-la-la-la-la

la-la-la-la-la-la

copyright © 2013 by Krista Detor. Tightrope Publishing

DAY FIVE – JULY 6, 2013

We've been sailing the Benjamin Islands, and I got another song today. This time, a harder one 'A little Misty' centered around my uncle. This probably won't make the album, but I spent half my childhood at my aunt & uncle's house. The garage was converted into a poker parlor, with the requisite tapestry of the poker playing dogs, a bar with fancy stools, boxes of candy bars and a refrigerator full of sodas and beer.

My aunt loved Johnny Mathis back then and I'll forever think of the two of them synonymously. *"Look at me.. I'm as helpless as a kitten up a tree."* She always finished the NYT crossword. I adored her. "You're so odd," she'd smile, at family gatherings, in such a way that I knew was the highest compliment.

They had an ornate pump organ in the poker garage that I played, pulling out all the stops. It was always a good place to be, what with the big hand-blown glass ashtrays, endless soda supply, and pinochle games that went well into the night and kids running room to room.

My cousin and I would go to the racetrack with my uncle and his friends sometimes. He was always happy, always scheming something, always smiling, always amazed; taking us aside to whisper: 'Here's a little money. Put it on Darby's Delight in the 5th' as he and his entourage headed out for general rat-packery. Funny how, more often than not, he kept the company of not just questionable, but completely reproachable, fellows. I tell myself he saw the best in everybody.

Maybe he just loved digging up a good story from under the rocks.

A Little Misty   on the boat   kd 7/2013

Heading to the horse track in shorts too short and
hopes that boys would notice
- hoping old men wouldn't
We got in big trouble for the red fingernails -
you look like floozies gonna land in jail
we'd paint it over pink at the ladies' room sink
but who in the world cares what old men think?

There were matching floor mats on the plush floor, red
wine leather and a white hot door
tickets from the racetrack tucked into the visor,
hidden on the ride home - women none the wiser
we were tooling down the highway
richest man I knew
was a high-rolling saint
and he was nothing like you

He had a big idea
he would make a million dollars
shelling souvenirs to strangers, visitors and trawlers
maybe mark a little territory. think up some commodity
that no one ever thought of before

And in the meanwhile, a whiskey
drink a little whiskey, while away the hours
while the world got tipsy
we'd pick a couple flowers
from a graveyard, wandering
sit a little while and watch the world go sprawling -

drink a little water from a hose and
think of those who never
thought of drinking water from a hose
and so it goes, and so it goes

In the backseat, we dreamed Tiger Beat dreams
of boys, dreamed boys, boys and boys
sometimes I dreamed a house
with long white curtains
I didn't know I dreamed of linen,
nothing that I knew was certain -
I believed I dreamed of some place
better than 'because' -
but I dreamed like a side-effect;
I only dreamed I was ..

I held a hand-held mirror in the pale green bathroom,
drawing a line where my brow line had been
right above the bright blue shadow that was brand new
bought at the drug store, maybe, yeah I stole it
but I was singing Misty,look at me, I'm Misty,
there I was with black and blue eyelids, Misty
and I was doubting everything,
I was doubting everything
I was doubting everything
I was doubting that ever thought was true
singing.. Misty, dreaming of you

While he was dying, we ate pizza
and I needed to tell him that I WOULD see him

that he'd STILL BE there, yes, he WOULD,
when I came back in the Fall.
Did he see it on my face –
because I never felt so selfish
should have hidden it all better,
everything was afraid of,
I should have hidden everything,
I should have hidden everything,
I should have hidden everything,
should have hidden everything,
should have hidden everything,
should have hidden everything
that ever was at all
I should have hidden everything,
but .. I didn't
and when I came back, he was gone, he was gone.
It was Fall and that was all

tooling down the highway
richest man I knew
was a high-rolling saint
and he was nothing like you

He was nothing like you

Look at me, a misty kitten, dangling from a tree
like a hand, from a glove
I don't know a thing about love
it's all… misty

CHAPTER 5: BRIDGES

Art: Courtesy of Won Sook Kim

A Little Misty didn't make the album. I tried to work it

out, musically, but it kept channeling *Subterranean Homesick Blues*, and despite my genre-crossing, I have limits. For almost a month I tried to work around melody line, to modify, edit.. I couldn't find it. I was saddened that not all 4 songs would find their way to the *Flat Earth*. *Misty* will find its way, somewhere, somehow, down the road. But for the time being, I went back a handful of years to

BRIDGES - one of the first songs Dave and I ever wrote

together. It never fit an album before this one. The chorus never sat right with me so I re-wrote it, and now it does.

A handful of years ago, I sat in my own house one town over, scrawling a lyric line while someone I love, but have not seen for years, sat next to me, only vaguely aware of me, drinking wine from a big bottle. She alternately laughed and cried as she told stories from our mutual past and lamented some of her own. I only hear rumor of her now, despite the entwining of our lives.

I wish I heard more. I might forever wish I heard more.

From: Krista Detor
To: Arbutus Cunningham
Sent: Fri, June 17, 2011   10:42:11 AM
Subject: crab apples

I been in the deep waters, Luella.
No sun for days.
My nose is out now, I suppose. Just the tip.
I don't want to dive down in the isolated and hermity
but I haven't wanted any semblance of
human company for the longest time and
have begun dreaming of the days when
small children breach the perimeter of my
crabgrassy yard and I can hurl both
cackley threats and crab apples at them
simultaneously..

Coffee?
Signed,
the crooked man in a crooked little house

From: Arbutus Cunningham
To: Krista Detor
Sent: Sat, June 18, 2011   9:15:42 PM
Subject: crab apples

Waiting on the rain.
Which has maybe changed its mind,
gone off to Germany where it isn't needed.
I want to go to Far Norraway where I am not needed and live
beside a blue fjord, fish for cod over the side of a small dory,
knit wool lace on skinny needles with fish-stinky fingers at
night, never talk to anybody.
Not a mumblin word.

Yes coffee.
I will be happy to see you.
We can talk about fjords and things we like.
I am not in a hurry.
After the weekend there will be home made ice cream left over
from Fathers Day.

Sven Svensonsdatter

LANDSCAPES

From a window
once saw Dakota sunset
red tomato
spilling juice into
the thirsty hills

Full moon
over flat land
white skull hollow inside
no blood
splintered stars
sudden bits of ivory
falling

Brown skin
white dress
a memory of wings
far blue hills
round to the eye
as the breasts
of a woman
the sun held
inside

Buffalo grass
curling tighter
nearer to the
earth
river bed
colored stones
eyes of dead men
never blinking

Flat plain
dustcloud
tumbleweed
bones
bones
bones
the wind crying
a wounded animal
bleeding
no more blood
bleeding still

- Doug Lang, Outlaw Memory

If I gave a blessing for every blessing I've been given
Kindness would blossom around me every day
But I seem to have come too late to the party
And we know it ain't worked out quite that way.

- Rick Reiley

Sea Glass

An Indian liniment bottle,
hurled violently into the channel
one night with an earthy curse,
fractures in slow motion
against the cobbled bottom.
The flask of female tonic that couldn't keep
four babies in a row from dying,
the empty rum bottle that slipped from
a sleeping fisherman's fingers
under darkening skies:
these, too, shattered to raw triangular shards,
and the restless waves shuffle them
among blue mussels, litter, and wrack.
Now a lump of harbour–sugar
gleams within your palm.
Sand has wintered the glass
to soft frost.
To be whole again....and yet
To lose one's purpose and be lost,
To roll a sad tale over and over again in your mind
till it's ground to a fragile glow.

–Betsy Johnson

BRIDGES

Krista Detor & David Weber

I've been looking, she said, for the doorway, she said
for the answer, she said, to the question
I've been drinking, she said, in my bedroom, she said
painting pictures, she said, of my children

I've been trying to find it for so long
that I think that the doorway is not where it used to be

CHORUS:
It's all water gone under the bridge,
it's gone under the bridge,
oh it's good and gone to places I've never been
Bridges are burned and fall down in the messes I've made
Burning bridges, the price I have paid

I remember, she said, in the desert, she said
never had to buy my own drink
Had a boyfriend, she said, he played football, she said,
called me 'beautiful,' she said, I think

I've been trying so long to forget him
that I think sometimes I never met him

BRIDGE:
Walk me over to the other side of the house
give me nothing to make me believe all of this
lead me to the place where I'll lay my head
give me something to make me sleep, she said

I'm a painter, she said, but I'm not sure, she said
why the canvas is white. Nothing's here.
They forget me, she said, an old story, she said
and I know from the things I don't hear

I've been trying to run my hands over and under it
someday, maybe I'll feel the color.
Trying to paint them for so long
that I think that the pictures
don't look like them
anymore

BRIDGES

by Krista Detor & Dave Weber

INTRO

VERSE 1

look-ing, she said, for the door - way, she said, for the ans - wer, she said, to the ques - tion I've been

drink-ing, she said, in my bed-room, she said, pain-ting pic-tures, she said, of my child-ren I've been

try-ing to find it for so long that I think that the door-way is not where it used to be (ooh -

CHORUS

ooh) It's all wa - ter gone un - der the bridge, it's gone un - der the bridge, oh, it's good and gone to

pla - ces I've ne - ver been Brid - ges are burned and fall down........ in the mes - ses I've made Burn-ing

copyright © 2013 by Krista Detor. Tightrope Publishing

91

bridg-es, the price I have paid ___   I re-

G#7   E   Aadd9   E   Aadd9

VERSE 2

Em   C   Em   C   Em

mem-ber, she said, in the des-ert, she said, ne-ver had to buy   my own drink   Had a boy-friend, she said, he played

C   Em   C   E   Aadd9 Am

foot-ball, she said, called me beau-ti-ful, she said, I think   I've been try-ing so long to for-get him   that I

CHORUS

think some-times I ne-ver met ___ him ___ (ooh - ooh)   It's all wa-ter gone un-der the

E   Aadd9   Am   F#7   (drums in)   E

Aadd9   E   Aadd9   E

bridge, it's gone un-der the bridge, oh, it's good and gone to pla-ces I've ne-ver been Brid-ges are burned and fall down

BRIDGE

Aadd9   E   G#7   A

in the mes-ses I've made   Burn-ing brid-ges, the price I have paid ___ Walk me ov-er the ___ oth-er

copyright © 2013 by Krista Detor. Tightrope Publishing

Bridges (3)

side of the house give me no-thing to make me be-lieve all of this lead me to the place where I'll

lay my head and give me some-thing to make me sleep,_____ she said

INSTRUMENTAL

I'm a

VERSE 3

pain-ter, she said, but I'm not sure, she said, why the can-vas is white. No-thing's here. They for-get

__me, she said, an old sto-ry, she said, and I know from the things I don't hear I've been try-ing to run my hand ov-

- er and un-der it some-day, may-be I'll - ll feel the col-or___ Try-ing to paint them for so long___ that I

copyright © 2013 by Krista Detor. Tightrope Publishing

93

think that the pic-tures don't look like them an-y-more...... (ooh - ooh) It's all

Aadd9　Am　F#7

E

CHORUS

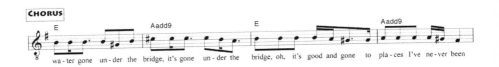

E　Aadd9　E　Aadd9

wa-ter gone un-der the bridge, it's gone un-der the bridge, oh, it's good and gone to pla-ces I've ne-ver been

E　Aadd9　E　G#7

Brid-ges are burned and fall down...... in the mes-ses I've made Burn-ing bridges, the price I have paid...... It's all

E　Aadd9　E　Aadd9

wa-ter gone un-der the bridge, it's gone un-der the bridge, oh, it's good and gone to pla-ces I've ne-ver been

Brid-ges are burned and fall down...... in the mes-ses I've made Burn-ing bridges, the price I have paid......

E　Aadd9　E　G#7　E

copyright © 2013 by Krista Detor, Tightrope Publishing

Day Six – July 7, 2013

So I'm up on the deck, and a melody and line jump into my brain. I can see the swoop of the cascade of the line as shape, rather than defined notes, around the words 'there's always somewhere left to go' – countering the dark night of the soul 'nowhere left to go' notion. It happened in that kind of surprising way. I'm looking out at the endless water, having sprung out of the berth this morning, slammed the Weber (grill) ball cap on my mostly matted and braided hair (I don't think I've showered in a while but not sure) and, hands on hips, blurted out, delightedly: "WHERE WE HEADED TO TODAY?" "I don't know," said, Anne, but we're going somewhere!" and there it was. If I were a dog, my ears would have perked at the whisper of a song..

I didn't actually care where we were heading because anyplace and everyplace is a good destination. And maybe the openness of the minute – my mind not attached to any particular task or order of events, and the song maybe found a crevice to seep into, like a mist.

This is a rarity, and the best possible song start for me, with no warning, with no intent. And all I had to do was get it down fast enough. If you don't grab it out of the air, it disappears 'like dewdrops in sand,' a lovely line George once wrote. And then you're sifting, sifting, but it diffuses instantly, gone for good.

Luckily, I grabbed this one fast enough. And then back up top to see if I could see land yet. But whether I could or couldn't - didn't matter.

CHAPTER 6: ALWAYS SOMEWHERE

Tightrope Records artwork by Hugh Syme

In all ways, ALWAYS SOMEWHERE came directly as a result of sailing the Great Lakes. A little chill in the air, sitting on the deck of the boat, I flashed on Ludington, a coastal village on Lake Michigan, where Miner, a good friend, has a family cabin that's been in existence since the turn of the 20th century or so, called "Buckeye."

Years before, I'd forwarded him an irreverent piece I'd written, loosely in the style of Robert Service. My father can quote Service tomes at the drop of a hat – especially in the presence of Tullamore Dew Irish whiskey, and he'd gotten me hooked years earlier. He'd sent me a mournful piece he'd written in Service-ese, I answered back, and also sent it to Miner, who I thought would get a laugh out of my effort. And maybe he did, but the piece he returned, built around Service's poem, *The Shooting of Dan McGrew* – a call and response that he'd written years before named, aptly, *Recitations* - was stunning.

And suddenly in my mind's eye, I'm there with him, an observer as he deliver s his father's ashes to the great lake. I'm there, on the back of the bicycle I imagine he's riding, his father's ashes in a hand-tooled leather satchel, heading into the icy wind, toward the infinite and unknown.

The song begins streaming into my head, and my laptop is dead, so I have to plug it in to get the song down before it leaves (they're like that) – only one cell phone works where we're anchored, still, I unplug it and try to slam my jack in, but in a frantic Carol Burnett comedy of errors I can't make it work and 'I'm really sorry about this, but I need to get this down.. help' melee. My hosts are patient people, alongside their pragmatism and intricate knowledge of the workings of plugs and jacks and such.

I got the song down, alone below deck, in a few minutes. It spilled out in the imagined voice of Miner's father, speaking the words I might speak to my own children – of infinite possibility, the limitless world beyond the pale, the best we can hope to be in the flash of light/time we're here - the best advice I could give myself that I haven't often enough taken.

My hope spilled out between the words. My always holding, despite the ice and surge, hope. But true to form, for me, it had begun years before in a quippy-ish toss-off.

Prison Without Walls

There was a time I swapped pennies for dimes
And then had to leave on the run.
Been shot at a bit, but I've never been hit.
You've got to be tough when you're dumb.

Without her by my side, it's a mighty rough ride
And it don't make no sense at all.
'Cause, I'm doing' my time, without reason or rhyme
In a prison without any walls.

Me and the boys are a pretty tough bunch.
Crooks of the white collar kind;
Bankers and farmers and preachers and such,
Just tryin' to hold onto their minds.

We try to stay busy but there ain't much to do
'Cept worry about what's happenin' at home.
We walk in circles and we keep in touch
By calling collect on the phone

I have floated down stream in a salt river flood,
With my belly so damn full of booze,
That I ended up with my butt in the mud.
It was a hell of a night for a cruise.

I sat on the curb while my house was on fire...
Seems some moron was smoking in bed.
And the fool, you see, looked alot like me,
So, I've taken up chewin' instead.

They say I printed some currency notes
And I heard they didn't look so bad.
They not only took my house and my boats,
They took everything else that I had.

But possessions aren't what's botherin' me
'Cause I knew I was due for a fall.
It's me sittin' here like a fool, you see
In a prison without any walls.   *– Bud LeRoy 1991*

Pondering Robert Service
in the 100 Year Flood

A hundred year flood, now we're covered in mud
and never such soggy grass mown -
Oh, the teeth of the storm took a perilous form
with a bite only few had 'ere known

Bearing down like a wife who's been handed a knife
and a husband with wandering eye -
it cut a gash in the land, like the heart of the man
and then left without saying goodbye

oh, we all heard the warning, but who, in the morning
could dream what the siren rang true!
of a day, as we know, the damn thing'll blow -
and it only means lunch is past due!

So some lounged in the evening with aperitifs, dreaming
of fireflies, moonbeams and such -
Then to bed with a book, and nary a look
at the radar - *bad news is too much!*

Nestled in like dumb squirrels in the hollows and burls
of our bedrooms and couches (and gutters)
we woke to the sound of the sky falling down
and the wind tearing off all the shutters

And we cowered and clamored and uttered *Alas!*
and some hid 'neath the beds in bordellos
in hotels and motels in the black underbelly
and the company of questionable fellows

At the Vid and at Legends where legends are made
on the laps of Night Moves clientele -
and we scuffled and shuffled and prayed for the end
of the storm that might send us to hell!

While the good people clung to their children
and sung songs of teapots and spiders and stars -
there are those, it is said, who would rather be dead
than to give up their stools at the bars.

There are those of the wild, who've not seen a child
as they'll n'ere see the harsh light of day -
for they sleep with the sun, and a loaded handgun
to banish the demons away.

And they chew up the thunder and never crawl under
a shelter, umbrella or roof -
And they spit out the lightening - a spectacle frightening
for even the bravest – 'tis proof

that the devil is well, and that storm came from hell
and maybe the black blood of man -
Still, for us who lived through it, no drink will undo it -
nor one thousand bags all filled with sand –

and we'll speak of this night - and the teeth and the bite
and the rivers that run where none had -
to our grandchildren whisper - *I nearly lost my sister -
but then that, maybe, wouldn't a been so bad..*

- kdetor 06/11/08

RECITATIONS

MY FATHER RIDES ABOVE AND BEHIND ME
IN A HAND-TOOLED LEATHER SATCHEL.
WE ARE HEADED NORTH AND HOME.

>*Were you ever out in the Great Alone*
>*when the moon was awful clear*
>*and the icy mountains hemmed you in*
>*with a silence you most could hear?*

I AM TAKING HIM TO THE BIG LAKE TO
SWIM WITH THE COHO,
CUTTHROAT AND BROWNS.
TO KEEP A PLEDGE KNOWN, BUT NEVER SPOKEN.

>*Now a promise made is a debt unpaid*
>*and the trail has its own stern code.*

IT'S A NEW YEAR'S DAY AND A MICHIGAN DAY,
BITTER COLD AND CLEAR AS A BELL.
THE WIND IS BLOWING HARD NORTHWEST,
WAVES POUNDING AT THE SHORE,
THE ICY SPRAY DRIVES ME BACK,
I TURN FROM ETERNITY'S DOOR.

>*A pal's last need is a thing to heed*
>*so I swore I would not fail;*
>*and we started on at the break of dawn;*
>*But God! He looked ghastly pale.*

UP THE BEACH, AT THE STEEL
I CAN REACH THE RIVER KNEELING.
HERE, WITH MY HANDS, I COMMIT HIM
TO WIND AND SAND AND WATER.

*Yet 't'aint being dead -- it's my awful
dread of the icy grave that pains.*

ASHES BLEW ONTO MY HANDS, MY SKIN
TURNED GREY FROM WHITE.
I WASHED MY HANDS, I WASHED MY HANDS
AS LONG AS I COULD BEAR.
ASSURED OF HIS DELIVERANCE COMPLETE,
I STOOD   WITHIN A PRAYER.

- Miner Seymour, 1991

In the summer of 2012, I'd finished reading Woolf's *Orlando* and Fitzgerald's *Gatsby*. *Orlando* was an effort (worth it) but *Gatsby* had me immediately at 'what foul dust floated in the wake of his dreams,' and never let go.

I started writing *There Are Tracks* - a song that still might find its voice somewhere, stealing lines from the two books, and trying to weave an ambitious notion of two enormous and complex literary characters from different novelists having a conversation. It turned out differently than I'd imagined – taking stock of myself, I suppose, and the cynicism I'd adopted – referencing Woolf's 'ditchwater' (the stuff of political argument) also her 'precious conceit,' and 'wild abandon' with Fitzgerald's 'foul dust' as the backdrop. And then I set Miner in the midst of it, in duality - map of the Great Lakes in his hand, and the mining for treasure.

As *Always Somewhere* was streaming in like mist through the crevices, I went back and grabbed from *There Are Tracks* a couple of the notions that would flesh out the heart of the song. It was done and written in about 30 minutes.

And several years.

There are Tracks   kd 6/12
Says Orlando to Nick

Saw it once and I didn't see it again, didn't see it
What does it matter what does it matter if I see it?

Bent low by a ghost and now look at me -
barely breathing

I gathered up my thoughts and I packed em in a box
but I left it open
Despite what they say, what I say,
I'm eternally hoping
And I'd have danced if I could on the splintered wood
and left it all unspoken

But there are tracks,
I see them in the foul dust floating

I painted on the wall, a vine on the wall
above the landing
Came cracking through the wall, black stems and all
called it *wild abandon*
Precious conceit, paint on my feet
all I had a hand in

I scrawled messages to the unbelievers, unbelievers
served ditchwater cocktails,
ten-penny nails to receivers
Bent low by the muck and the rust, and look at me
how could I be her?

But there are tracks, I see them, like pearls in winter

What's the thing you whispered -
a pale flag twisting upward?
in the dust, faintly lettered:
you can be so much better

There are tracks, I see them in the foul dust floating
There are tracks, I see them in the foul dust floating
I do not look away when it's your hand I'm holding –
tracks, I see them in the foul dust floating

There are lines, I see them, to the hearts unloading
light, I see it, all the hearts unloading light,
bleeding light into the dust that's floating
there is love everywhere in the foul dust floating

ALWAYS SOMEWHERE

Krista Detor 07/2013

Don't let the shadows bend you low
because somebody tells you so
Believe in what you know you know
there's always somewhere left to go

The truth won't always set you free
but neither will a lie, so be
a better man than you thought you'd be
because you know you know
there's always somewhere left to go

it's hidden in a miner's map
and in a ten-cent photograph
so maybe, turn the key and laugh
because you know you know
there's always somewhere left to go

Instead of asking how and why
set out to find the bluest sky –
beyond the pale, it's my oh my,
and nowhere that you know
and there's always somewhere left to go

Believe in love and second sight
remember, they're not always right -
the ones who say you've got to fight
and never walk away

Believe in what not knowing brings
believe in why the caged bird sings
expect a thousand happy things
no matter what they say… because

110

hidden in the wake of dream
the darkness floats, but what might seem
the worst of all and everything is
blinding, beautiful
blinding, beautiful
blinding…
beautiful.

It's not enough to wish her, wish her –
4th of July, and you might miss her
so do it now, go on and kiss her –
oh you know, you know
there's always somewhere left to go

ALWAYS SOMEWHERE

by Krista Detor

INTRO

(Guitar)   Don't

VERSE 1

let the shad-ows bend____ you low____ 'cause some-bo - dy tells_____ you so____ Be-lieve in what you know

____ you know, there's al - ways some - where le - eft____ to go____ The

VERSE 2

truth won't al - ways set____you free   nei-ther will____ a lie, so be   a bet-ter man than you thought____you'd be be-cause

____ you know you know   there's al - ways some - where le - e -eft____ to go____   it's

VERSE 3

hid - den in_____ a min - er's map____ and in a ten - cent pho - to - graph so

may - be turn____ the key and laugh____ be - cause you know   you know   In - stead

copyright © 2013 by Krista Detor. Tightrope Publishing

VERSE 4

of ask - ing how and why set out to find the blue - est sky be - yond the pale, it's my oh, my, oh,

no-where that you know there's al - ways some-where le - e-eft to go Be-

VERSE 5

lieve in love and sec - ond sight re-mem - ber, they're not al - ways right the

ones who say you've got to fight and ne - ver walk a - way Be - lieve

VERSE 6

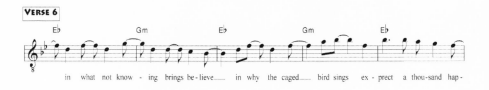

in what not know - ing brings be-lieve in why the caged bird sings ex - prect a thou-sand hap-

- py things no mat - ter what they say Be-cause

copyright © 2013 by Krista Detor. Tightrope Publishing

VERSE 7

hid-den in the wake of dream the dark-ness floats, but what might seem the worst of all and ev - 'ry-thing is

blind-ing beau-ti-ful blind-ing beau-ti-ful beau - ti - ful

beau - ti - ful

BREAKDOWN

It's not e-nough to wish her wish her 4th of Ju-ly you might miss her so do it now, go on and kiss her

oh you know you know there's al - ways some-where le - e - eft to go

(ouu ouu)

copyright © 2013 by Krista Detor. Tightrope Publishing

It's Limerick Wednesday!

A married man from Aberdeen
Took his ring off when e're he was seen
By the lassies and ladies –
The Marys and Sadies –
And all other girls in between! –   1/4/2012

It's Gone with the Wind Limerick Wednesday

"As God is my witness, " she vetted
"I'll never be hungry or Rhetted"
"Frankly my dear,
I don't give a damn, hear?
'Twas on the damn Yankees I betted!" –11/28/2012

It's Last Dance Limerick Wednesday!

The mirror ball spun and it glittered
in sequins, the pretty girls skittered
the Bee Gees were primped
and Travolta was pimped
and the whole time, not one of us Twittered
                              –09/04/13

Day Seven – July 8, 2013

Mosquito Cove.

We're under attack. Having stumbled upon a deserted and pristine cove, astonishingly void of any other sailors, cruisers or power-boaters, we've armed ourselves and are hoping to get through the night

This is the first brutally hot night of the trip, but, unaware of what was about to befall, we spent much of the early evening in relative comfort, watching the beautiful sunset reflect pink and orange onto the water and algae-covered rocks. We re-supplied yesterday at Little Current and have plenty of wine, beer and ice to get us through the next three days.

What we don't have and didn't think we'd need, is an assault weapon that shoots millions of tiny little mosquito-sized explosives at one burst. We've gone below deck to try and escape the onslaught, but every time we shore up an entry point, the mosquitoes find another. As if they're nano-bots, constantly responding to a new set of parameters by evolving brand new algorithms.

We've tried to distract ourselves by playing Scrabble, with the Captain and I trading occasional cold vodka shots to adapt to what has now become a nearly air-tight sauna. The Weber ball cap will barely contain the gigantic dandelion puff of my ratty, red hair, and I stopped caring on Saturday. Or Sunday. One of those days. Periodically, Anne or I jump up and clap unwitting mosquitoes to death. The Captain realizes the folly and doesn't bother. We're all covered in OFF, and he says we're battling 'raindrops in a tsunami.' I know he's right, but I do the ridiculous clapping mosquito dance anyway. They're mocking us. Can't he see that the mosquitoes are mocking us?

If we don't make it through the night, having perished from suffocation, OFF poisoning or anaphylaxis due to millions of mosquito bites, the unlucky discoverers of our lifeless sailing ship may think they've stumbled into a lost chapter of Lord of the Flies – *CHAPTER 13: Too Bad the Tourists in Mosquito Cove Suffocated Before They Could Discover the Lost Boys and Save Simon & Piggy.*

CHAPTER 7: FINE PRINT

Gilbert & Bacon 820 ARCH ST. & 40 N. 8th St. Phila.

me, in my last life.

FINE PRINT evolved over time, in the same way that much of *Flat Earth Diary* did – in spits and starts, misfires and mining expositions.

I have boxes of my grandmother's jewelry. She was the woman who'd put, immediately upon receiving any gift, a piece of masking tape on the bottom of said gift or gift box with the date and the name of the person or family who'd given it. Over a 50-year period, she made sure and certain that there would be no squabbling after she was gone.

There was, of course. Squabbling. Squabbling over trinkets, squabbling over the small savings she'd painstakingly put aside for her children and grandchildren. People grasping for meaning, significance, and the toaster cover tailored around the top half of a legless Barbie doll – tailored just so that a crocheted Scarlett O'Hara gown of sorts flowed from the doll, down snuggly over the rectangular Sears 2-slicer, and there stood Barbie next to the bread box, in courting gown and matching crocheted hat, forever awaiting Civil War Ken.

She left me books and dime store jewelry, a few trinkets, and a hat with a small feather plume in it. I stood no chance at the toaster barbie, so I let it go.

But I'll never forget the road trip she and I took my freshman year of college. It was an unwilling trip on my part -

I couldn't imagine anything worse, really, and had planned on listening to loud mix tapes, drinking endless diet cokes and smoking at least a pack of Marlboro Lights over the solo 13 hour drive from my house to the university. Despite my well-crafted and tear-filled arguments, my father insisted, and away my grandma and I went.

I'll be forever grateful for the insistence. We talked for all the hours on the road – in a way that no other situation had ever afforded us, nor would again. She was so candid. She'd been a 'big girl' – hearty German/Norwegian farmer stock, had married young (not for love – she never thought herself 'pretty' and he was a mean drunk), and that had made her harder than I imagine she ever wanted to be. She was somewhere in her late-60s at the time of our adventure, and she seemed to have this spark of renewed interest in the remote possibility of romance. As if, after decades of hard work, raising seven children essentially on her own when their father died young, she'd looked up and allowed herself to glance, however fleetingly, at the possibility of storybook love. I'll always remember the way she spoke it.

Years later, long after she was gone and the Barbie in her faded ball gown had moved to the shiny formica counter top of one aunt or another, I thought of my grandmother, as if in a snapshot - wearing the hat with the small feather plume –

and how some of us won't ever be fitted for crocheted dresses, won't be the first one the men tip their hats to, but somewhere, someone will maybe see how we're set apart, *and the fine print on my heart.*

The song took some digging, and once again, Dave's riffing on his guitar in the living room breathed life into it. Victor Wooten got it on its feet.

Digging for the Fine Print

Fine Print Mining Expedition #1

Where's the Art   10/12/12

Will you ever find a man to suit you
Sidle up and salute you?
Find a man to fill the holes
In your walls and cheeses, and your holy soles
Where's the art?
That's the missing part
What's missing.. is your **heart**

You oughta watch a sad movie and see if you feel it,
Get to a church and see if you kneel it
But **blind as a bat,** one thing is true -
You don't care about one thing that isn't you

Fine Print Mining Expedition #2

<u>Are you Missing Me</u>   1/29/13

Tell me, is it raining - would I be complaining
Tell me, are you missing me?

Did you paint a mystery - in a train car, maybe
where you are - Are you missing me?

Do you tip your hat to girls in confetti and oyster pearls
and tell me, are you missing me?

With the wild things on the road side –
did you pay for a bus ride
and write, write that you were missing me?

**Men don't tip their hats to me –
Flamingo pink, my lips, don't see
my shiny feathers,** are you missing me?

Fine Print Mining Expedition #3

Am I shortsighted, Molly?   10/6/2006
Cause I can't see what you see
How the fence runs long
farther than Butcher's oak tree

Cause I can't see beyond you in the orchard
Can't see beyond me –
Would be king of the world
Dressed up like a girl
with an apple in hand
I may have taken the fall, but **they don't know who I am**

Fine Print

Krista Detor   2/20/12   Kdetor/Dweber music 2/8/13

Don't bother to say that
you're just another - blind as a bat
The fine print is where the words start
and there's a fine print on my heart

I'm a rare bird in this instance –
a high flyer.
Insistence won't do.
Where's the art?
When there's a fine print on my heart

I wear black cotton gloves
watch the men tip their hats -
they see a little turtle dove
but I paint my lips
flamingo - pink as - flamingo

Don't bother with blue note.
The warble in your throat is dry
and lemon tart
and there's a fine print on my heart

I wear black cotton gloves
watch the men tip their hats -
they see a little turtle dove

I've sewn in black feathers
to my hats and my sweaters
and maybe he'll see –
how I'm set apart
And the fine print on my heart

FINE PRINT

by Krista Detor & Dave Weber

copyright © 2013 by Krista Detor. Tightrope Publishing

126

copyright © 2013 by Krista Detor. Tightrope Publishing

127

The Poets

The Poets

I could take you for a ride.
Wear your hat 'cause it might rain.
We'll send someone up ahead
to throw flowers in the lane.

- Art Heckman, *Flowers in the Lane*

Why they fly is a mystery to me
they've all got Google on their goggles
so it's not the view they see.
They're high, so high
on China's latest toy
but down here on my bicycle
I'm just an ugly Earthling boy

- Michael White, *Ugly Earthling Boy*

Some say geodes were made from pockets of tears
trapped away in small places for years upon years
Pressed down and transformed
'til the true self was born
And the whole world moved on
like the last notes of a song
A love letter sent without return address

- Carrie Newcomer, *Geodes*

Day Eight – July 9, 2013

We hiked in the Turnbull islands today. All of the 'islands' are rocky outcroppings, covered in trees, red algae, and in this case, wild blueberries. Only accessible by boat.

Greeted by some exuberant and drinkin-at-10-in the-morning co-eds, we made our way as far as we could through the unmarked trails and paths, gathering tiny blueberries everywhere we saw a patch. They were so small that you'd have to collect for hours to have any meaningful amount, so we ate them as we went.

We got there in the dingy, paddling. The boat was anchored a good distance off shore and I was certain I could paddle a dingy. I've been canoeing plenty, and though I've not generally been the rear, steering unit of a canoeing duo, how hard could it be?

Two paddles, going backward, plenty hard. Going forward was worse, and either way, I ended up rowing Anne and I around in circles, while other boaters looked on, bemusedly, and I laughed like an idiot. It was funny.

I seriously don't understand why spatial relations of all sorts are so difficult for me to grasp. It can't be a failure of my genetics because I come from a family of engineer-types. I'm the only one who breaks into a cold sweat trying to translate the two-dimensions of a basic road map into three. Regardless, through an incredibly complex route of figure 8s, circles and accidental moments of straight-lining it, we got to the island and back to the boat.

It reminded me of being at my Aunt Alice's lake

house when I was a teenager. The afternoon I tried taking my cousin's canoe out alone - but it had a high arcing curve at the bow, and it kept catching the wind coming off the water, driving me back, spinning me around. I fought it for a while and then gave up - just sat and let the wind spin me gently to shore. I was a slow-spinning helicopter seed falling from a maple tree on a warm summer day.

A song showed up - 'Hear That' - a snapshot of my sometime reckless late night, teenaged excursions, and I think I can safely say that I now have an album. Can't believe it!

I don't know why this trip is calling on so much adolescent imagery. Maybe because my father was a fisherman. Maybe because this trip is an adventure, It's strange to be bombarded by things long put away.

In the meanwhile, we've roughed out Flat Earth Diary some, playing music up top during the day and below at night. I wonder what the passing boaters think, as they drift by our musical trio - cellist, guitarist, and me with the Casio or accordion. Sailing the Traumfanger. We could be anybody. Maybe an avant-garde German ensemble, practicing for the Royal Albert Hall. Makes me want to cultivate a bad German accent.

CHAPTER 8: MARIETTA

Ophelia Exhumed, c. 1993

MARIETTA is the renovation of a song I sang in my post-college band, *Ophelia Exhumed*. I know. I laugh now, too. But at the time, it made perfect sense. But then, so did *Eraserhead* in the right frame of mind.

The song, 'The Ghosts of Peach Street,' on the *Mudshow* album, refers to an *'antebellum casualty at the end of a southern street.'* As I wrote the song, in my mind's eye I sat in the shotgun shack across the street; the sometime residence of Rattlesnake Bob, whose beloved was Marietta. The place was a hovel where varying Monroe, LA bands would practice, smoke cigarettes and drink warm beer and hard liquor. While we practiced, I could look across and sometimes see the dark and sultry Carol, sitting on the porch swing of the Peach Street house; cherry red lips and long, black hair. I played the piano in her parlor once, kudzu creeping through the walls and down the chandelier.

I'd moved to Louisiana with my then-husband, George, to be near his family, after he was discharged from the Army and we'd returned from Korea. I'd spent a year or so in Seoul with him, just out of college, teaching conversational English and piano, and residing as musical director at the theatre on the military base.

In his late 50s at the time, I was introduced to the legend of Rattlesnake Bob upon arrival, as either musical genius or glue-sniffing ne'er- do-well, who could periodically play guitar like Robert Johnson's drunken, Cajun uncle. Generally both. Marietta was.. well, the best way to present Marietta is to recount the story that was told to me by a bandmate:

Seems Marietta's brother, whom she lived with, along with some untold number of their kin in a house a block or two over, had been seen pushing his lawn mower, motor chugging, around the block, with an oblong, aluminum foil-wrapped package on top of the engine. After the 3rd time the mower rumbled past his front porch, my bandmate called out:

"Whatcha' you doin, Buddy?"

"Heatin' up the garlic bread!" yelled the grinning lawn mower pilot, affably.

So. She was a pin-curled flower in a colorful bunch, that maybe collectively got by on the wits of an average one. I'll never know. On the other hand, Rattlesnake Bob had a crackerjack intelligence, strung out and sweaty, calling out directly the gods of inquiry, postulation and purgatory.

The darkness that must have surrounded their relationship is self-evident and shows up in the original lyric. Bob really was addicted to huffing solvents. I saw him do it once, through a fuzzy, beer-glossed haze. These years later, I replay it and it takes on a *Mr. Toad's Wild Ride* cliché that surely is a product of time and imagination - the room shifting around all of us, ala David Lynch's forays into *Twin Peaks* episodic madness; sticky heat and loud music pulsing through the crumbling walls; Bob laughing uncontrollably, and then shredding some guitar solo.

But Marietta remains the innocent in my lingering narrative. She came out once to see *Ophelia* play at Enochs, the bar that we and all others of the era frequented, so that she could hear 'her' song. When we'd finished, she smiled sweetly, said, "I loved it," and then left, Bob escorting her out - gently holding her by the elbow – chivalrous, adoring. I never saw her again. We played at ear-bleeding levels, surely indecipherably, and thankfully for that, because all Marietta knew was that someone had written a song about her. I suspect that if she'd read every word of the song, she'd still have only enjoyed the fact that a song had been written called 'Marietta.' But I felt as if I'd exposed the soft belly of someone utterly guileless, however couched snugly in metaphor, and it felt unkind. The fact that she'd never know of the violation was no consolation.

Years later, Marietta morphed into something other - something somehow embodying the murkier aspects of my own Missouri Synod youth. I assigned her the role of witness to that which I couldn't view directly. She became the solitary, the idée fixe, the dog-eared dream of the King James past.

I kept Marietta in Ouachita Parish, though.

We'll always be there.

In My Last Life

kdetor 10/18/2007

In my last life the curtains were drawn and the ocean's waves landed like giant's feet on a hardwood stage. I buried bits of wood, carved with my name and birth date all over the back yard, and sat at a quiet table in a playhouse, nameless birds chirping bits of secret messages. I never tried to understand them. I made mud pies and dreamed of baby dolls with hair that grew longer and shorter with the turn of an arm.

I called across the brick wall that separated my neighbors from me - the girl, Ginger, and the boy, Butch - and I heard the sound of engines revving in the driveway across the street. Rough men laughing, boys bursting through the prickly shrubs with footballs and fingers held in V's, for the peace signs people flashed in parades and marches, and the cigarettes they'd smoke later, behind the garages.

In my last life, monsters made daisy-shaped paw prints in the bathtub and the curtains were drawn. The streetlights came on at 8:30 in the summer. Bikes were strewn on lawns and dogs slept restlessly, chained to backyard trees and immovable posts, dreaming doggie dreams of children wandering near, who'd drop bits of half-chewed hot-dog and bun; endless dreams of fields of steak-shaped rabbits, and long, long rivers where dogs swam to the sea..

I dreamed a giant spider on the wall, they said, when my teeth were coming in, and three years later, told my mother that my grandmother had died, when, as the story goes, thousands of miles away, she had. My aunt whispered, conspiratorially, when I, a teenager, sat gazing over her shoulder at the New York Times crossword puzzle; where I sat in her rococo living room, with the thick gold shag carpet and reproductions of porcelain Marie Antoinette and Louis the XIV. *'Didn't your mother tell you? It's true.. you told her before she got the phone call..'*

My only prophecy, but still, dead on. No one ever asked for an encore.

In my last life, I floated down the river Seine on the back of a porcelain dog, while stone- faced boys lit firecrackers & cigarettes in the deep, black culdesaq. I watched the mothers, as I drifted by, pulling honeysuckles, one by one, from the vines and pushing them into the empty garden beds.

.

Marietta & I kdetor & GDetor 01/93

Marietta drinks her coffee from the broken cup
And reads the Sunday paper from 1982
I stand up long enough to lie again and reckon a familiar
sound - flannel brushing white legs, hidden black and blue

I'm dreaming of Marietta in a church in New Orleans,
she's speaking of shapes and rattlesnakes
and God's own incongruity
Marietta with the pin-curled hair
It was only me who put her there while we were sleeping
she'll say she felt my breathing
but my breathing, Marietta, is all that's keeping me here

Marietta smiles on Sunday and she never says a word
Smiles at the Sunday paper, sometimes she smiles at me
I stand up long enough to lie again, reckon a familiar sound
someone talking to her – no one I can see

I'm dreaming of Marietta in a church in New Orleans,
she's speaking of shapes and rattlesnakes
and God's own incongruity
Marietta with the pin-curled hair
It was only me who put her there while we were sleeping
she'll say she felt my breathing
but my breathing, Marietta, is all that's keeping me here

Marietta & I (revised)   kdetor 03/05

Marietta drinks her coffee from the broken cup
Always from the same cup and
I fall into it and break at the glue line
I fall in - I am broken roses on her china cup

She reads the paper, wet rings on the paper
leaking through roses down onto the paper
And I am undone in the sweet sticky rings
And I am undone by the transient things

Chorus:
I stand up long enough to lie…
I tell her she's pretty - she always believes me

I know of a sound unlike any other,
It's hollow and ashen and whispers of sin
It's subtle inflection, a thing left unspoken -
The brush of the flannel against her dry skin

I stand up long enough to lie again…
I tell her she's pretty - she always believes me

Coda

MARIETTA

Words & Music by Krista Detor Music by George Detor

Marietta drinks her coffee from a broken coffee cup
Always from the same cup and I am always falling in
Coffee drips onto the table through the broken cup
And I am undone in the sweet, sticky rings
I am undone in the transient things

Light falls from the air on Marietta when she's sleeping
Shrouds and thorns and crosses burning on the hill
and I am dreaming

Marietta smiles on Sunday if I am very quiet.
She smiles at the Sunday paper, sometimes she smiles at me
I might get up and walk across the room –
and maybe I won't.
I won't if I don't,
and the sun'll come up like the sun always does

Light falls from the air on Marietta when she's sleeping
Shrouds and thorns and crosses burning on the hill
and I am dreaming

> I know of a sound unlike any other,
> It's hollow and ashen and whispers of sin
> A sound in the night unlike any other
> The brush of the flannel against her dry skin

And I will not leave this room or the spot on the mirror
where I breathed a fog and it stayed there for years and years
little xs and os
and I watched myself sleeping
and crying and dreaming
and I have tried, but Marietta and I won't be leaving

Light falls from the air on Marietta when she's weeping
Shrouds and thorns and crosses burning on the hill and I am
dreaming

of Marietta in a church in New Orleans
I'm speaking of shapes and rattlesnakes and
God's own incongruity
Marietta with the pin-curled hair
It was only me who put her there
while we were sleeping.
She never felt my breathing

but my breathing, Marietta
is all that's keeping me here

MARIETTA

Words & Music by Krista Detor
Music by George Detor

copyright © 2013 by Krista Detor. Tightrope Publishing

won't if I don't and the sun-'ll come up like the sun al-ways does

CHORUS

Light falls from the air on Ma-ri-et - ta when she's sleep-ing Shrouds and thorns and cros-ses burn - ing

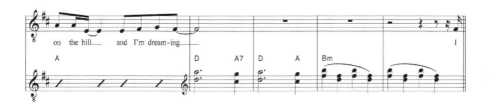

on the hill and I'm dream-ing I

BRIDGE

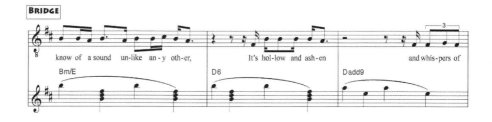

know of a sound un-like an-y oth-er, It's hol-low and ash-en and whis-pers of

sin A sound in the night un-like an-y oth-er The brush of the flan-nel a-gainst

copyright © 2013 by Krista Detor. Tightrope Publishing

146

INSTRUMENTAL

her dry skin

F#m Eadd9 Dadd9   A9sus   A   G   D   G   Aadd9

G6   D   G△   A   Asus   And I

VERSE 3

G△   D/F#   G   D/F#   G

will not leave this room   or   the spot on the mir-ror   Where I breathed a fog   and it stayed there for

A   G   G   D/F#   G

years   and years   lit-tle 'X'-s and 'O's and I watched my-self sleep-ing   and cry-ing

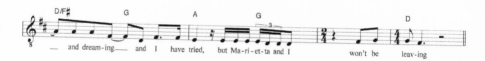

D/F#   G   A   G   D

and dream-ing   and I have tried, but Ma-ri-et-ta and I   won't be   leav-ing

CHORUS

A   G   D   G

Light falls from the air on Ma-ri-et - ta when she's weep-ing   Shrouds and thorns and cros-ses burn-ing

copyright © 2013 by Krista Detor. Tightrope Publishing

on the hill___ and I am dream-ing Of Ma-ri-et-ta in a church___ in New Or-leans, I'm___ speak-ing

Of Shapes and rat-tle-snakes and God's own in-con-gru-i-ty,___ yeah Ma-ri-et-ta with the pin-curled hair___

it was on-ly me___ who put it there While we were sleep-ing she ne-ver felt my breathing my

breath-ing___ Ma-ri-et-ta is all___ that's keep-ing me here

copyright © 2013 by Krista Detor. Tightrope Publishing

148

Day Nine – July 10, 2013

The Perfect Storm hit today. I woke up to the boat bobbing, small waves splashing and a slate gray sky.

I nabbed a motion-sickness scrip before I flew to India in the Fall of last year, and had the inexplicably genius idea to bring it along. If I hadn't, I can't even imagine the clean-up of the mess I'd have personally made as the nightmare day progressed.

We have a show in Egg Harbor in two days so we had to head West into 80-knot winds and 40 foot seas.* I was convinced that death was imminent, as the bow of the boat crashed down, over and over, falling from the high crests of angry waves and threatening to bust into splinters as it smashed down. It didn't help that we'd actually hit a hidden, uncharted rock the other day, jutting out off of a peninsula under the surface in Mosquito Cove. Who knew what untold damage had been incurred? It didn't help that my hosts had only had the boat a couple of months because how could they know what kind of battering it could take?

But mostly, it didn't help that I had the genius idea to go below deck and make us sandwiches, to quell the queasiness. I hit 'the wall' down below, watching pickles slide off mayo-slick bread. If you've ever been seasick, you know the moment of no return. I got back up top with the food as soon as I could, but it was too late, and the waves edging over the boat and soaking the seats didn't help. I gulped down the soggy mess, mumbled some greenish apologies, and went below to my

*It might have been 25 knots and 8-foot seas.

berth, where I chewed up two more seasickness pills and curled up into a ball on the bed, pillows at my head and feet. There would be 8 hours of sliding starboard to aft, as the boat rocked violently.

Finally, I had to use the head (boat talk for bathroom). It was unavoidable. I held on tightly as the boat careened, taking one slow, sickening step at a time. I made the fatal mistake of looking out the small window at the enormous grey waves, endless against the black sky, and for a full minute I knew that they would need to call the Coast Guard to get me off the boat right now. Get me off the boat. NOW!

But as I came out into the cabin, I looked up to the deck and saw Jim casually crack a beer. He was relaxed, holding a handrail with one hand, sipping a brewski with the other. Like we were pleasure cruising off of St. Tropez. In that moment, I knew we'd survive. Unless, of course, he was sucking down his very last beer and wanted to savor it before the Kraken ate us for mercilessly making fun of the boat name.

Turns out he wasn't. Eventually, he headed south, out of the storm, and life got back to relative normal. It means that tomorrow we'll have a long haul back to U.S. waters, but it's absolutely worth it. And I told them I'm glad for the experience, but I will never sail in 40-foot seas again. Never. Under any circumstance. Ever. Even to escape the Kraken.

CHAPTER 9: HEAR THAT

My friend, Brian sneaking me into The Palomino, L.A. on a late night adventure

HEAR THAT is unlike anything I've written. It's

rebellion, recklessness - a search for meaning and identity. It's *She's Leaving Home*, with no witness and no discovery.

It's sneaking through the quiet house late at night, listening for my father's breathing, careful not to excite the dogs, and slipping out the sliding glass door to the backyard, where I'd scale the block wall, and skip, fearless, like a tightrope walker, across the top of it to some friend or another waiting with a car, a 6-pack and an adventure.

The thing that's striking me most about this handful of songs is that they're more personal than I'm ordinarily comfortable with. All decent love songs have to spring from the personal, I'd think. And I've written more than my share - but we've all, all of us, been in love at one point or another. The inceptions and outcomes, whatever they be, are generally universal. But more often than not, I write character pieces. I'm a character writer. The process of imagining someone, some subject; fleshing out his face, her hair, car, walls… coloring in the view from his window, the last thing she remembered before the scarlet light turned blue. That's the writing I like to roll around in and make a Twister game out of when the moon is full and maybe no one will read it.

It's easy juggling a character's flaws, bad judgments and triumphs. Trickier, juggling personal mementos.

Some of them are sharp.

HEAR THAT

on the boat   Krista ddetor 7/2013

I
Hear that?
the sliding glass door slid shut
and they'll never know what's what
I snuck out for good that's what, I did

Hear that?
the clock with the figurines stopped
they kissed wooden kisses and stopped
and froze right around 3 o'clock, around 3

Hear that?
It's the sound of the room as I left it
the dogs as they yipped when I left it
and no one around to regret it, but I said it, I said it

Hear that?
the bottle of half-drunken wishes
tossed into a full sink of dishes
and pouring away like a river, pouring out

II
Hear that?
the white hum of tv & bad blues
the smell of the blood in the bad news
the smell of the life I did not choose, I did not

But hear that?
It's the grind of the gears over gravel -
like a mad swarm of bees, it's the rattle
of snakes in the trees, hear them rattle, hear them

III

Hear that?
the break in the circuit, the silent
at the end of the song- all is quiet
no one around to deny it…. no one

But hear that?
the sound of a sliding door shutting
and they'll never know what was whatting
I snuck out for good and I'm running, ah for good

Hear that?
the sound of the power lines crackling
you right next to me .. and we're laughing
and I know what I'll be and I'll have it
with no one around to regret it
so I said it
Hear that?

Hear That?

Words & Music by Krista Detor

copyright © 2013 by Krista Detor, Tightrope Publishing

CHORUS 2

said it I said it____ I said it Hear that? the bot - tle___ of half drun - ken

whi-sh - es tossed in - to___ a full sink of di-sh - es and pour-ing___ a-way like a ri-ver,___

VERSE 3

pour - ing___ out___ Hear that? the white hum of T - V___ and bad blues the

smell of___ the blood in___ the bad news the smell of___ a life I did not choose, I did___ not___

CHORUS 3

Hear that? It's the grind of___ the gears ov - er gra - v - el___ like a

mad swarm of bees, it's the ra - a - a-tle___ of snakes in___ the trees, hear them ra - tle,___ hear them

VERSE 4

___ Hear that? the break in___ the cir - cuit, the si - lent___ at the end of___ the song all___ is

copyright © 2013 by Krista Detor. Tightrope Publishing

CHORUS 4

qui - et   no one   a - round to de - ny   it   But hear   that?   the

sound of   a   slid - ing   door shut - ting   and they'll ne - ver know   what was   what - ting   I

CHORUS 5

snuck out   for good and I am   run - ning,   ah   for   good Hear that?   the

sound of   the po - wer   lines cra - ck   ling   you right next to me and   we're laugh - i - ng   and I

know what I'll be   and I'll   have   it   with no one   a - round to re - gret it

so I said   it,   hear   that?

copyright © 2013 by Krista Detor. Tightrope Publishing

161

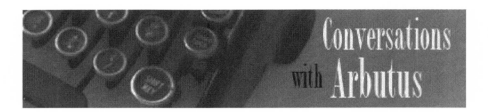

Sent: Sun, May 29, 2011 9:04:12 AM

Arbutus –

My dog died last night - probably hit by a car. Dave and I both at a birthday party and we got the panicked call. Ran home - he'd been gone for hours. Died on the back step by the studio door. My heart's all broken up. I loved that crazy devil dog. Wretched evening, a house full of crying girls, Dave beside himself and lost, and me trying to hold it together despite the nasty blueberry wine from up the road.

I woke up this morning before anybody else and drug Azrael's pillow out to the bonfire, put it up on the sticks, stacked like a pyre. I looked over toward the wedding wall and there was a beautiful red horse standing next to a dappled pony eating crab apples under my tree, both of them looking at me with swishing tails.

The air was so still. I didn't know whether they were really there..I actually blinked a stupid movie blink. like I'd stepped out of my door onto a movie set, and cameras were rolling.. so surreal. For whatever reason I said hello . They didn't leave. I turned and tiptoed in, then ran upstairs, got Dave and two apples. We walked out to them and they came right up to us and ate apples from our hands. The big one walked up onto the porch and tried to get in the door like Pippy Longstocking's horse.

I went in and woke the girls.. delighted & baffled kids fed horses apples & carrots in the yard for the next 45 minutes. We found the horse owners down the road. they came and walked them home. It was a kindness from the Creator that I won't soon forget.

And it's a funny old world.

I miss my dog. If your mama believed he had a soul, I'd ask her to pray for it.
xo K

162

All dogs have souls, enormous souls. Dogs know this, they wag and smile even when in great pain, they put up with all manner of bad dog food (brought to you by those wonderful people at Monsanto), myths (a common belief less than a hundred years ago was that dogs, in fact most animals, were so inured to pain that they did not require anesthesia), being romped on by small children, chained up in tiny yards, used as subjects of brutal experiments, dogs recognize kindness as the one rule and command, not always or even often reciprocated, but that's not part of their equation. Dogs are kind in and of themselves; they greet us with joy; they share our griefs without ever requiring that we share theirs (though they appreciate when we do); they watch out for us; they speak the only universal language of love, the true deep affection that abides and does not demand (unless you are cooking fish and then they want some, too, of course they do; food is love, tangible, juicy, and wonderfully satisfying; the wise person, said Lao Tzu thousands of years ago, feeds people). They make homes out of houses, and offer sweet (according to the perceiving ear) music to the night's mystery. They keep in touch: with each other, with the dead possum by the side of the road (they honor the dead), with us, with certain important trees, rocks, mud puddles, dogs need to know what's happened, what might happen, what lives under the porch steps. They are vigilant, and can be trusted to chase away threats: cars, blatting trucks, skunks, potato beetles, coyotes, earthquakes--Teddy O'Neill knew about that earthquake 3 years ago way before I did. He bumped the bed; stuck his nose in my face; finally barked, which he almost never does, at 4 in the morning. Get **up**! Something weird is shaking! Dogs really do protect and defend, like policemen are supposed to do, but dogs do not wear cultural blinders (and they disdain guns as a sign of weakness); race, class, and ability levels mean squat to them. I left out gender, which is extremely important to dogs, though male dogs do not ever patronize females on account of if they do, they get their asses whupped. "Anthropomorphize" is an ugly word invented by humans to indicate our self-proclaimed exalted status, but we do not, in fact, impose human characteristics onto dogs. Back before someone wrote that we were only a little lower than the angels, back when nights were long and the stars far away, we knew better. We knew we were animals, our chances of survival dependent on what help the neighbors (ravens, dogs, cats, wolves, bison, salmon, hummingbirds, dragonflies, the whole animated world, in fact) could or would offer us. Most human people have lost the ability to become seals or salmon, to slip into another skin and exalt creation with fins, fur, feathers (I still miss wings). Dogs are our sure connection to that memory of when we were all animals together; they are our partners, our friends, always to be cherished. Always.

When a good dog dies, the word goes out, people come by to pay respect to honor, fidelity, great-heartedness. I figure the horses for mourners, neighbors who came by to say Azrael that good dog was loved and respected, and will be missed. Didn't he struggle home, wounded and broken, to take up his station by the studio door, close to the hands that cherished him, the hearts that loved him? And didn't you do the right thing, put his pillow up on sticks, feed the mourners apples, recognize the difference great loss will always make in our lives?

I will go put the special geode with the crystals in the flower pot Teddy likes to pee on as a small memorial to that good dog Azrael, may he run free. My heart goes out to you and yours at this sad time.

love,
Arbutus

I do.

Day Ten – July 11, 2013

We're back in U.S. waters. Stopped at Rogers City to check me back in to Customs, and then back to Cheboygan. We'll shower, eat dinner in town and pack up the boat tomorrow. It's been an amazing trip.

I don't want it to end.

We have two shows – one tomorrow in Egg Harbor and one Saturday in Milwaukie. We're going to actually play Flat Earth. See how it flies. I haven't fully set Always Somewhere or Hear That to music. I know the notion of both of them – recorded snippets on my iphone of the melodies that I'll lock down when I get back home. I haven't given up on Misty, but I don't know where it sits.

Will I keep this time alive in myself as I head back into civilization and the jackhammer pound of deadline? I want to. But I want to do a lot of things, and my personal discipline has proven pretty ineffectual to this end. I get swept up in the pending, passing, fictional 40-knot gales of drama and apprehension, and by the time I come to, it's been weeks and I've forgotten the sound of small waves lapping against the sun-bleached dinghy, forgotten that life wasn't always what they'd have us believe it is.

We didn't always run as fast as we could to produce and accumulate as much as we could so we could prove, and never prove, our human worth. Aren't we all exhausted? All of us looking for water in the diamond mines. One confused with the other… At least, for now, Jim just called 'Fivesies!' and we've got frozen water enough left for two extra-dry martinis (& lime rind to twist. Doing my small part to fight scurvy. Today's only accomplishment.)

CHAPTER 10: HONEY DOWN A STRING

My parents, in a little photo, in a silver frame

My attempt to capture the fleeting moment became

HONEY DOWN A STRING.

There's a photo of my parents in my hallway. It's a tinted black and white, sometime in the 1960s, not long after their wedding, when every single thing was possible. The tinting left their eyes bright blue, lips a little too-pink, a peach blush on the cheeks.

Despite the artificial color saturation, something extraordinary comes through - as if they're lit from inside. They are captured in a wondrous and wide-open moment - life has become very good for both of them: They have each other, they have eternal possibility in a span of endless years. They've lasso'd the moon and are swinging on stars.

I live in the country, surrounded by corn and wheat fields, deep, old woods for muddy miles, and thick layers of stars on summer nights. In my mind's eye, I set the tinted couple at the rutted bend at the end of my road, on a walk, holding hands.

I followed behind, back far enough that they'd never know I was there.

Postwar child:
Woolacombe Beach, Devonshire, 1946

The old photo,
turning brown
reminds me:

> Pushing and shoving each other
> the boys chant, "I'm the King
> of the Castle. Get down you
> Dirty Rascal."
> But I'm too busy to play,
> packing handfuls of sand
> into holes the incoming tide
> eats in our castle, then running down
> with the retreating foam to push up
> a sand wall against the waves'
> next surge

Didn't I know I was losing?
Soon parents would call us back
as the high tide swept towards
our picnic place, strengthening
the undertow – warning notices
posted along the dunes – that made
even wading dangerous, and disturbed
lumps of oil, from tankers
sunk during the war. In the photo
I can't see any oil stains on my feet
or hands, but by the end of each day
I was always sticky.

Who waded out and took this picture?
my mother would have been too busy
talking, flirting even, I realize now.

    I'm the only girl out here
    in the sharp wind off the sea,
    spray from the waves thrown
    in my face, like rain
    that threatens in the grey sky.

The other girls must have been
back at the picnic spot, still eating
their tea or making little shapes
in the sand with buckets and spades.

    My bare legs are smeared with sand,
    my bare toes dig in, I can feel streaks
    drying on my face where I've tried
    to brush the hair out of my eyes.
    Seaweed is carried in on each wave;
    we pound the dark tangle
    into the sides of our castle. The pods
    make squelching sounds as they split.
    When the big waves break, gulls flap up
    screaming. We shout at each other, "Here."
    "No, here, stupid!" "Oh, look out."
    and the boys start throwing
    wet sand at each other.

    I'm left alone on top.
    -- the sea washing around my ankles –
    sinking as the castle falls apart,

and that's the moment,

> my face serious, still holding
> a handful of sand,
> the wind blowing my hair ribbon
> loose

the picture was taken.

Someone else's father,
hearing my mother's increasingly strident
"Antonia, come here!" waded out,
snapped me and when a wave pulled back
took my hand and ran up the beach with me.
Then, I'd have picked up my towel,
put on my shoes and socks, helped my mother
shake crumbs off our blanket,
trying not to listen as she scolded me loudly
embarrassing the others,
and, upset, trailed behind
as everyone walked to the hotel, chatting.

At the top of the dunes
-- I   can see myself now — I stopped
and looked back.
The sea had covered it all

- Antonia Matthew

IN THE GEOGRAPHY OF LONGING

This terrain with its horizon
of grain and clouded sky
stretches past the last

of light's edge, ending in dusk
and questions; where exactly
do the lines of demarcation fall,

how far to north, and when
the compass needle points
how accurate is the reading?

Yearning is a wordless song
wind at dawn, trees leaning
towards winter like a silent
empty house where purpose
is a guard at the door.

I clean windows. Water plants,
polish cupboards with lemon oil,
wash each dish, dry it, put it away,
check the clock
-- *Shana Ritter*

Despite the minute I felt I'd actually grabbed hold of, *Honey Down a String* almost didn't make the album. I wrote it on guitar, and am sheepish about public performance on an instrument that exists to exacerbate my inability to effectively translate 3-dimensional abstractions. I shelved the song but continued to play it, when I was alone (and never, ever in the presence of guitar players).

But as we were considering possibilities, after I'd come back from the Traumfanger excursion, Dave asked me to play it for him. I did. He said, "let's go record it." I hesitantly agreed.

In the studio, guitar in hand, I gave it a couple of tries. I didn't like the feel, the lack of precision. I wanted him to take over. But he said, "try it on piano." I was skeptical, but I did. And it worked. We were both happy with the outcome.

Months prior, I'd heard the Helber Sisters downtown in Bloomington, where I live. Vicki was (successfully!) battling cancer, and there they were, these three lovely women, who'd been singing these beautiful, old-time and Appalachian pieces in 3-part harmony for years. It was sublime. When I'd finished recording *Honey*, I could almost hear their voices echoing, between the lines.

It's a small town. I tracked them down.

Honey Down a string

Krista Detor 05/2011

sun on wheat
against the olive hillside
just about a mile wide, about a mile away

are tinted lips
and a pale blue shadow
in a little photo, in a silver frame

lovers speak the untrue
and someone hopes it will do
that someone never was you

ginger ale
left out on the walkway
probably been there all day, warm as morning tea

smooth and sweet
like honey down a string, oh
it's all that I can think of, thick and sweet must be

lovers speak the untrue
and hope that someone will do
that someone never was you

at the muddy mile, in the rutted bend
maybe sit a while – til scarlet sky is blue again
and stars come out

Don't you carry on so carelessly
when you are so close to me, when you are so near
cause someone's singing *Autumn Leaves*, oh
outside someone's window
darling, can you hear?

lovers sing the untrue
and someone hopes it will do
but that someone never was you

starry-eyed in the scarlet light
like the photograph - not a trace of pride
wishing on a star

someone's singing *Autumn Leaves* oh
outside a window
darling, as they fall

smooth and sweet, like
honey down a string, oh
it's all that I can think of

when I miss you most of all

.

Honey down a String

Words & Music by Krista Detor

INTRO

(piano)

VERSE 1

Sun on wheat a-gainst the o-live hill-side just a-bout a mile wide a-bout a mile a-way are

tin-ted lips and a pale blue shad - dow in a lit-tle pho-to in a sil-ver frame

CHORUS 1

Lo-vers speak the un - true and some-one hopes it will do that

some-one ne-ver was you

VERSE 2

Gin - ger ale left out on the walk-way prob-'bly been there all day

VERSE 3

warm as morn-ing tea Smooth and sweet like hon-ey on a string, oh

copyright © 2013 by Krista Detor. Tightrope Publishing

copyright © 2013 by Krista Detor, Tightrope Publishing

copyright © 2013 by Krista Detor. Tightrope Publishing

Day Eleven – July 12, 2013

On the road around the U.P. to Egg Harbor, Wisconsin for tonight's show at Woodwalk. Love the place – it's an old barn, converted into a beautiful music venue and gallery on an amazing piece of land, run by amazing people.

The boat is docked and locked down, and real life starts again. This is a more familiar passage of time – the barely noticeable hours slipping past with the county lines and gas stations. I can go hours in a car without even checking a clock now. I tell people it's like being a truck driver. It's a paradigm shift and within the paradigm, you're an object in motion moving a little faster than you ordinarily do.

You adapt. You also get used to Subway and have your order down, pat, when the girl in the disposable gloves asks if she can help you.

That's also part of the paradigm.

Dave will play percussion on Flat Earth tonight, and I'll read the words off a printed sheet, and we'll hope that the audience is kind, that the July evening is cool, and that the gods of inspiration smile benevolently, having missed all the angry voice mail messages from the Kraken*, regarding the irreverent stowaway aboard the Traumfanger.

---

*I'm not a sea monster, but I know where they drink. I've gone a couple of times, but I can't hold my breath long enough to win the pool game.

CHAPTER 11: FLAT EARTH DIARY

The cabin of the Traumfanger and my piano

FLAT EARTH DIARY: From the minute I met her and saw the product of her brilliant mind, Won Sook Kim has been an inspiration. I've spent a good bit of time in her home and studio, seeing new works emerge, unexpected shifts in media – from paint, to clay, to her latest cast bronze wall sculptures which dance in the moving shadow of moving light. Without fail, I leave with an inspired sense of possibility (not to mention the lingerings of an amazing meal and the just-enough sweetness of prosecco. She's an artist in the kitchen as well).

I'm lucky. I can call this gifted and generous woman a friend of mine, and in this particular instance, that friendship allowed me to jump into the star field of her beautiful imagery; into the contemplative solitude of her subject within the beautifully lyrical framework of the unknown; the whispered blessing floating just below the surface of the infinitely *possible*.

I'd like to think the album speaks something of the possible, because, despite appearances, I am eternally hopeful.

That poets that unknowingly contributed to the piece have since graciously offered for reprint the poems that I borrowed lines from, and in this way Flat Earth Diary is absolutely the most collaborative solo album I've made. So many people contributing resource to its physical inception, and so many perspectives involved in its conception – a handful of writers, all standing on different patches of ground, writing the tumbling clouds as they fall into the pond; writing the whipping wind and the white-throated birds; standing, all of them, naked at the margin.

The Poets

Unworthy Eyes

Is poetry best described as
a) inspired choral-song in time of war
b) a roomful of hallelujahs
c) finely-crafted iteration, or
d) just more blah-blah-blah flung unrepentant
into bumper-to-bumper traffic?

Well... yes.

Also, a house of cards,
and of enslavement, sacred narration
and its bastard commentary.
The opening between a rock and a hard place.

Every poem's intent reveals itself
reluctantly, incrementally,
in fragments of meaning— those signs
and wonders laid down in the back pages
of notebook or paper napkin.

In our 3 a.m. insomnias. Seekers all,
we are taken in by the words. Acolytes,
messengers, desperados—
worshippers hell-bent on transforming
the mundane into the astonishing.
Surely this is one of Heaven's marvels,
the unrestrained mating of vowel and consonant,
the muzzled love and veiled allegory.
Is it desire – or our infatuation with desire –
that poetry inflames?
Again, yes.

We long for the muse of incongruity,
to laugh with heads whipped back,
to create *ex nihilo* something
greater than ourselves. Slaves every one,
we long for majesty, are often plagued
with narrow thinking and the less-
than-transcendent view.

Poetry is false prophet and quick study,
everything we throw into the fire, sanctification
of all we regret, e) all of the·above.

I can always tell when you've been writing,
my beloved says sweetly, *your face
looks like it's still holding the dagger.*

Okay, I'll cop to it – I've been running
the wild streets. Looking to cut loose and bring ruin
to my own 2-faced cowardice. I can't bear
to have it said of me:

What happened to the woman
who brought us this far?

Too bad she's stuck on that rocky
mountain-top again, frightened for her footing,
grown tired of waiting for what she didn't
know was possible.

Friends, I'd rather throw myself
out of a window than abandon this tent
of outstretched desire. Rather set my head on fire
than be bound by my own limited vision.

Surely I can fill the page with vernacular
and not be tamed by it. Surely I can
do better than this. I long to be faithful witness
to all life's face-to-face,

but to wait up here alone—

Surely God could remember me,
whisper on occasion: here's the word
you're searching for, the extraordinary
standing naked at the margins
of your mind.

Look.

This way.

Perhaps I will (after a lifetime), though
it's more likely that –
like the rest of Earth's disappointing creations –
I will unveil my eyes only after
the letters have already inked themselves,
disorderly & drunk, revealing
what is to be found among the shards

– Susan Swartz

THOSE WHO HEAR IT

I write my poems
with thoughtful intent,
weighing every word,

rant and rave in letters
to politicians and editors,
enumerating facts in logical order
and few care, or even remember
beyond a day
what I might have said,

while the **white-throated** sparrow
sings each spring,
and those who hear
its small, clear stream of song
remember for years.

t. Tokarski, Mar. 2010

STOPPING BY TRAFFIC ON A BUSY MORNING

(A tribute to J. Kander with help from R. Frost)

Whose words these are I think I know
for Jenny told me so.
She will not mind me stopping when I should go
in the rushing traffic's flow
to hear the radio fill up with rondeau.

Now some may think it queer
to listen in this noisy atmosphere
between the mall and the belvedere
on the darkest morning of the year.
She gives **her harnessed words** a shake
to make sure there is no mistake.
The only other sound's the sweep
of easy verse and downy phrase.

The words are lovely, dark and deep
and Jenny has promises to keep,
classics to read to make us weep
and volumes to go before she sleeps
and volumes to go before she sleeps.

t. Tokarski, Nov 04

RELEASE

Trees sway with the wind
in variable waves of grace
as the clouds send down
their rush of rain.
Freed to the land, the shower
is an audible scrim, a gray wash
over leaves and limbs.
The flowers in the fields,
heavy with wetness,
droop as if in thanks
for what they have been given,
for what they have become,
there seems no separation
of earth and sky,
of mind and meaning,
of the wind and the rain,
all is free, released and mixed
in the madness of wonder
in common miracles.

t. Tokarski, Jan. 2013

The Perfect Poem

Has a full moon float
over it and two stars,
one
            cascading…

A stray mutt runs through it
barking his spots into oblivion
while on green hillsides
fleeceless sheep whimper.

In the perfect poem
**a roseate cloud
cartwheels over a fence
crashing into a pond** full
of amnesiac peepers leaping.

The exceptional rhythmic
expression offers the sound
of a lone stallion
neighing for his errant
donkey lover.

In the perfect poem
a Havan cigar
flames into life,
but this stogie gives off

no carcinogens
just thick white smoke
smoke that readers
must crawl through

before the perfect
poem swoops low
singeing our eager
yet vulnerable fingers   - Doris Lynch

The Flat Earth Diary

on the boat

Krista Detor 7/2013

At the end of the summer, and the fruit's in a jar
will you hum another wish, waiting on a shooting star
connecting dots to dots in blackness
giving faces to the beasts
thinking fondly of black waterfalls
with pools of stars beneath
off the edge, the water falls . . . to pools of stars beneath

At the end of the wishing
and the pierce of ice that's cracking
while the clouds tumble, crashing,
and then fall into the pond
will the wind go on whipping
like a jealous sister, whipping
til you find the tiny opening
between what's here and what is long gone
At the end, see what's here and what will always be gone

And there at the end, with the strange bells ringing, ah
will you repent and join the singing, ah
or stand on the flat earth, still believing, ah

At the end, will they say
you wrote it down and then imploded
will you leave behind philosophy- stanzas to be quoted
about your uncle playing poker
beneath a tapestry of mongrel poker faces –
he gave you all your best lines, you'll say
at night that dog still chases you and bites
The dog bites.

At the end, will love be muzzled when
 a knock comes at the door
will the bells ring out
'cause Sunday morning's rolled around once more -
will you plague yourself with ponderings
of the black and bloodless sky
(why'd the chicken cross the road?
It forgot that it could fly)
At the end, when you could simply fall in love
will you? will you?

I am naked at the margin on an island of swans
the boat is named *Redemption* – but the vessel I am on
is called *The Madness of Wonder*
and by the harnessing of words
I'm playing a pump organ
to the silence of white-throated birds
to silence
and unrepentant birds

In the end, the song was simply too long, and, despite much
bidding, bluffing and winking, my poker-playing uncle
waved goodbye and went back to the sunny California
highway, where he drives forever the big white Mercury with
red wine leather seats, listening to the 'Oldies but Goodies'
station, and stopping at the 7-11 to buy us ice cream
sandwiches for no reason at all.

FLAT EARTH DIARY
kd revised 09/13

At the end of the summer, and the fruit's in a jar
will you hum another wish, waiting on a shooting star
connecting dots to dots in blackness
giving faces to the beasts
thinking fondly of black waterfalls
with pools of stars beneath
off the edge, the water falls . . . to pools of stars beneath

At the end of the wishing
and the pierce of ice that's cracking
while the clouds tumble, crashing,
and then fall into the pond
will the wind go on whipping
like a jealous sister, whipping
til you find the tiny opening
between what's here and what is gone
At the end, see what's here and what will always be gone

And there at the end, with the strange bells ringing, ah
will you repent and join the singing, ah
or stand on the flat earth, still believing, ah

At the end, will they say
you wrote it down and then imploded
will you leave behind philosophy- stanzas to be quoted
how you plagued yourself with ponderings
of the black and bloodless sky
(why'd the chicken cross the road?
 It forgot that it could fly)
At the end, when you could simply fall in love will you?
will you?

197

And there at the end, with the strange bells ringing, ah
will you repent and join the singing, ah
or stand on the flat earth, still believing, ah

I am naked at the margin, on an island of swans
the boat is named *Redemption* – but the vessel I am on
is called *The Madness of Wonder*
and through the harnessing of words
I'm playing a pump organ
to the silence of white-throated birds
to silence
and unrepentant birds

And there at the end, with the strange bells ringing, ah
will you repent and join the singing, ah
or stand on the flat earth, still believing, ah

FLAT EARTH DIARY

Words & Music by Krista Detor

INTRO

(acoustic guitar)   (mandolin)

VERSE 1

At the end of the sum-mer, and the fruit's in the jar...... will you hum a-no-ther wish, wait-ing

on a shoot-ing star con-nect-ing dots to dots in black-ness giv-ing fa-ces to the beasts think-ing

fond-ly of black wa-ter-falls with pools of stars be-neath off the edge the wa-ter falls to pools of stars

VERSE 2

.... be-neath   At the end of the wish-ing and the pierce of ice that's crack-ing while the

clouds tum-ble, crash-ing and then fall in-to the pond will the wind go on whip-ping...... like a

copyright © 2013 by Krista Detor. Tightrope Publishing

jeal-ous sis-ter, whip-ping 'til you find the ti-ny op-en-ing bet-ween what's here what is gone At the end,

CHORUS 1

see what's here___ and what will al-ways be gone gone And there at the end, with the

strange bells ring-ing, ah-ha,___ ah-ha, ah-ha will you re-pent___ and join___ the sing-ing, ah-

ha, a-a-ha___ or stand on___ the flat earth, still___ be-liev-ing a-a-a-ha

VERSE 3

At the end, will they say you wrote it

down and then im-plo-ded will you leave be-hind phi-lo-so-phy stan-zas to be quo-ted how you

plagued your-self with pon-der-ings of the black and blood-less sky (why'd the chi-cken cross the road? It for-

copyright © 2013 by Krista Detor. Tightrope Publishing

got that it could fly) At the end, if you could on - ly...... fall...... in love? Will you? Will you?

CHORUS 2

Will you? Will you? Will you? And there at the end, with the strange bells ring-ing, ah-ha,...... ah-ha, oh-

ha will you re - pent and join...... the sing - ing, ah-ha...... a - ah - ha...... or

stand on...... the flat earth still...... be-liev - ing a-ha-ha-ha

INSTRUMENTAL   **VERSE 4**

I am na-ked at...... the mar-gin on an

is-land of swans the boat is named re-demp-tion but the ves-sel I am on is called The Mad-ness of...... Won-der through the

harn-es-sing of words I'm play-ing a pipe or-gan to the si - lence of white-throa-ted birds to si - lence and

copyright © 2013 by Krista Detor, Tightrope Publishing

201

CHORUS 3

un-re-pen-tent   birds   (band comes in)   And there at the end, with the strange bells ring-ing, ah - ha,
                              B   E

E   A   B   G#m
_____ ah-ha, oh - ha   are you gon-na re-pent and will you join the sing - ing, ah - ha   a - a - a - ha

A   F#m   G#m   A   C#m   F#m   G#m   A   C#m
_____   or stand on___ the flat earth___ still be-liev - ing   stand on___ the flat earth___ still be-liev - ing or

F#m   G#m   A   C#m   C#m   B   E   A/E   E
stand on___ the flat earth still be-liev - ing   a-a-a-h-ha   a-a-a-ha   ah - ha_____   ah - ha_____

E   A/E   E

copyright © 2013 by Krista Detor. Tightrope Publishing

Day Twelve – July 13, 2013

It's 2½ hours from Egg Harbor to Milwaukie for the show tonight. We're listening to some of what we recorded before I left. Filling in the missing pieces. Flat Earth Diary went over really well last night. That's a hopeful thing. I see the arc of the album now – the shape of it. Snapshots from my past – fairy tales, the old swiss cuckoo clock with the kissing boy and girl, the race track, Lawrence Welk and dime store jewelry.. Peach Street.. my wedding day. The road map from there to here and then forward off the edge of the earth, where I hope to ride a waterfall down, down and out…

No net.

There never was one.

Chapter 12: Blowing Kisses

The piano I learned to play on

BLOWING KISSES was the result of a collaborative experiment a handful of years ago, with my friend, composer Jim Krause.

He writes beautiful melodies for guitar and cello, and this one, *Madeleine Bay*, caught my ear, listening while I was driving down the road one winter day in 2009. I'd heard it a hundred times, but as it goes, this time I could hear a 2nd melody weave through and around the lines, like thread. I got home fast enough to get the whole thing down.

The lyric itself is the recounting of a snapshot, again: An interchange at an airport, as I put my oldest daughter on a plane to visit her father. In the car on the way, at 8 years old, she'd asked for the first time why we'd divorced. I did my best to explain in the - 'some things aren't meant to be and isn't it great that he's so happy now and I'm so happy now, in relationships that work better for us? And you have two Christmases!' - recount of clichés and stutterings. But there never is a good answer.

What could I say? We're human beings, kid? We tend to marry when we're young and *immortal*. Forever is a long time and we have no real notion of what it will mean when we can actually glimpse the rim of the event horizon and realize we are completely unsuited to be together for the duration of the flight. Despite abiding love that never really goes away, despite years of friendship and years of hope, paradigms shift. When they do, sometimes there is collateral damage – but maybe the damage is worse if you stay when you shouldn't. The one thing that holds true is that there will be no paradigm shift that ever affects the way either of us feel about you. It's our biological and emotional imperative. We have to adore you. Forever. Period.

Maybe she'd have gotten it; even laughed a little. But she was 8, so I said, 'some things aren't meant to be, but we both love you so much' and put her on the plane. Just as she was about to enter the jetway with the flight attendant, she turned and blew me a kiss. I caught it and blew one back. She'll always be there, crossing the line from one life to another. And I'll be blowing her kisses all the way.

Blowing Kisses

kdetor   12/2009

You asked me once how I left it
It never ends, you know, so I said it.
I turned you around, across the line
'blow me a kiss,' I said, 'you are mine.'

And wars are won without a gun
if the words are pointed, every one
but despite the secrets we all keep
did you know stars burn on while we sleep?

While white sheets billow on lines
we still know that all that ever will go will go by
So there you are
and here I'll stay
But I will blow you kisses all the way

Sometime, some day, something goes away
But when we wake, we find the brilliant sun the same

So I write the story - maybe a lie?
But come whisper to me, and if you can, fly
from where you are
when here I'll always stay
and I will blow you kisses all the way

BLOWING KISSES

Music by Jim Krause
Lyrics by Krista Detor

copyright © 2013 by Krista Detor. Tightrope Publishing

VERSE 2

with-out a gun if the words are point-ed, ev-'ry one

but de-spite the se-crets we all keep did you know stars burn on while we

VERSE 3

sleep? While white sheets bil-low on lines, we still know that all that ev-er will go

VERSE 4

will go by So there you a-a-re he-

copyright © 2013 by Krista Detor, Tightrope Publishing

213

- e - re I stay But I will blow you kiss-es all the way

E△ A6/E G#m A G#m A B7 E A B E

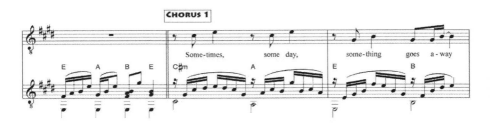

CHORUS 1

E A B E C#m A E B

Some-times, some day, some-thing goes a - way

VERSE 5

C#m A E Bsus E E/G#

But when we wake, we find the bril-liant sun the same So I write the sto-ry,

A E A B7

May-be a lie? But come whis-per to me, and if you can,

copyright © 2013 by Krista Detor. Tightrope Publishing

214

fly_____ from where you are when he - e-re I'll al - ways stay and I will blow you kis-ses all the

E   C#m   A   F#m   B7

way_____

E

copyright © 2013 by Krista Detor. Tightrope Publishing

215

Ocean Waves

When the big one would come
we'd make an "aw!" of anticipation,
our ocean Everest building height
over panoramas of lesser hills,
and in the lift and curl and bash just
for a moment we understand the urge
of the world in the unconscious
flip of its bicep.
I could almost encircle your girlish waist
with hands to lift you above the monster's gnash,
and your screaming giggles rose
over the breaker, joined
the chorus of the beachgoers.
And then the biggest one ever starts
far out, takes its thrill of time,
deceptively lightening gray to green
Still, we stood that time from the abrading
roll between sand and foam,
choking burn of ocean up the nose,
and I saw you fling your hair back
and with evolution-given instinct
stare ahead for the next wave, looking then
more serious, no giggles.
It's out there now, my dear girl,
and it'll push you under in whiteness and thrash,
it'll scrape the hide from you
so you'll get a glance at what's underneath.
I can report from the future you won't be
disappointed in what you find.

The sea has been digging at us forever;
the more it digs, the more it finds.
Eyes to seaward, my daughter.
The sand-pail days are not over
but from now on
the shore will be exploring you.

-Betsy Johnson

A Way

Earth's children grow
leave home
go away where
dragons roam

dragons fly aweigh
to lands on maps
filled with children grown
away from home

Hubble captures dragons
a way from home
away from children
aweigh in space

children young and old
pass away as dragons fly
where earth aweigh
finds a way
to roam

home

- *John Harrington*

Acknowledgments

My heartfelt thanks to everyone involved in the *Flat Earth Diary* Project - to the wonderful people who contributed and collaborated; to David for abiding faith in me, despite the incessance of my arguments; Aurora, Lena and Isla for being the most amazing part of every one of my days; to the friends and fans who contributed to the funding project; To Won Sook Kim for the use of her glorious art and to Thomas Clement for introducing us, and for wonderfully living by example; To Arbutus Cunningham for never letting me get too big-headed nor too loud-mouthed; to the Poets whose beautiful words I've reprinted - years of inspiration, thank you; to Anne & Jim for the constant inspiration and the sailing adventure that gave me space to let the thing wake up; to Margie for the wardrobe and a thousand smiles; to Peter Kienle for wonderful work on the lead sheets, and for contribution of brilliant lines when he least expects them; to Mo & Ben for smiles that light the room and pink-flamingo dances; to Willa Shaffer for holding my hand and answering emails that elude me; to Cathy & Tim for years of support; to Bud & Dyann for what will be the best stories of my life; to Miner Seymour for Buckeye & Recitations; to Frs. John & Pat at Tobar Mhuire for reminding me that there are secret gardens yet to be uncovered; to my cousin, Echo, who spent the red wine leather backseat years with me, listening to The Bee Gees and drooling over Robby Benson. To Robby Benson for coming to teach at IU and recording a piece at Airtime, so that I could email my cousin to crow about Robby Benson coming to my house! To my Aunt Lila for seeing something in me that not everyone did, and my uncle Andrew for showing me that life is exactly as happy as you decide it will be. To my parents for the piano, the lessons, and then the absolute unwillingness to let me quit the lessons, and to my mother for talking me out of dropping out of college because I was in love with someone 2,000 miles away; to my brother, Rob for his good soul and (thankfully) forgiving nature; to Ryan for living by example with bright eyes and endless optimism; to my grandmother, Wilma, for the trinkets, the red velvet box, the feathered hat and the books that I intend to be buried with; to Brian and Pam for keeping my piano all these years; to Sherrie for years of advice and Pam for walking the long road with me; to Mike Lindauer for years of generous travel and laughs; Andrew Peters for working tirelessly to promote me throughout the land; to Faith & Glenda for the priceless advice and shoulders for my cowgirl tears; to Robert Meitus & Thomas Kuhn for always taking my calls; to Dan Reed for being my hero; to Victor Wooten for teaching me the value of discipline; to Carrie Newcomer for being herself and encouraging me thusly; to the women writers that flesh out the beasts, serve up Indiana tomatoes and argue theology, and to everyone whose ever listened to or read what I've written - You've meant the world to me.

All works reprinted herein are done so with the
express permission of the authors, as listed.

You can find them all on-line.
They like to be found.*

---

*If you have any trouble, I know where they all drink. For a song, I'll tell you.